The PATH Of LIGHT

The
PATH Of
LIGHT

A Guide to 21st Century Discipleship and Spiritual Practice in the Kriya Yoga Tradition

ROY EUGENE DAVIS

CSA Press • Lakemont, Georgia

CSA Press
is the publishing department of
Center for Spiritual Awareness
Lake Rabun Road • Post Office Box 7
Lakemont, Georgia 30552-0007 (U.S.A.)
(706) 782-4723 Fax (706) 782-4560
E-Mail csainc@stc.net
Web Site www.csa-davis.org

Read a little.
Meditate More.
Think about God all the time.

Paramahansa Yogananda

PREFACE

In this book I have explained philosophical principles and guidelines to Self- and God-realization which have been taught for thousands of years by enlightened saints and sages. The subtitle, *A Guide to 21st Century Discipleship and Spiritual Practice in the Kriya Yoga Tradition*, defines its purpose. To comprehend the theme, read the text in its entirety, including the Glossary. Then read it more slowly. Apply the recommended routines and practices to your personal needs. Diligent, faithful practice of what is learned, will improve the quality of your life, enhance the clarity of your awareness, illumine your mind, and liberate your consciousness.

The text of Patanjali's *Yoga-Sutras*, an important treatise on superconscious states and spiritual practices written in India several hundred years ago, is featured in Part Two. Part Three is taken from the Introduction to my book, *The Eternal Way: The Inner Meaning of the Bhagavad Gita*. To acquire essential knowledge and for inspiration to sustain your spiritual practice, regular reading from these sources is recommended to all practitioners of Kriya Yoga. In Part Four, I have provided information about the teachers of this Kriya Yoga tradition and the methods by which the teachings are transmitted.

It was an early evening in late December, 1949, an hour after my arrival at the international headquarters of the Self-Realization Fellowship, in Los Angeles, California, when I first met Paramahansa Yogananda. Quiet, courteous, and somewhat reserved, he welcomed me with gentle affection and gave me his blessing.

After two years of study, learning, discipleship training, and intensive spiritual practice, I was ordained to represent this enlightenment tradition. As I knelt by his chair, my guru placed his hands on my head. I can still feel his touch and hear his clear, strong voice: "Roy, I ordain you a minister of God. Teach as I have taught. Heal as I have healed. Initiate devotees of God into Kriya Yoga!"

By offering this book to you, I am performing one of my spiritual duties. My earnest prayer is that you will experience a quickening of the Spirit of God in you and be inspired to right actions that make possible rapid unfoldment of your highest good.

ROY EUGENE DAVIS

Lakemont, Georgia
August 1, 1998

Contents

Part One

The Path of Light

ONE

Basic Teachings

Kriyas are intentional "actions" implemented to resist, pacify, and remove mental and physical conditions which blur, distort, and restrict awareness. The elimination of these conditions allows *yoga*—the restoration of awareness to its original, natural state of wholeness—to be realized. Spontaneous kriyas are the transformative actions which occur when soul forces are awakened and circulate freely.

Because Kriya Yoga practice purifies the mind and ego, clarifies awareness, attunes one with Nature's enlivening influences, increases receptivity to grace, and accelerates spiritual awakening that culminates in illumination of consciousness, I refer to it as *the path of light*. Because the philosophical principles upon which these teachings and practices are based are in accord with natural laws that can be discovered and verified by anyone, they are timeless and universal.

The highest and best knowledge we can apprehend is clear knowledge of God that unfolds from within the innermost level of our being. When God is actually known and experienced, and we are established in this realized state, rapid awakening through the final stages of spiritual growth spontaneously occurs.

Truth seekers who are new on the path—and even

13

some more experienced devotees—may believe that many years of arduous endeavor will be required of them before they can be awake to Self-knowledge and God-realization. For some devotees, further study for the purpose of improving their understanding of themselves and their relationship with the Infinite will be necessary. They may have to engage in extensive self-training and undergo psychological transformation that will contribute to improved mental function and emotional stability. They may have to adhere to a regimen of spiritual practice to develop intellectual powers and awaken intuitive capacities. For others, whose powers of perception are already more developed, a change of viewpoint that allows clear apprehension of their true nature and the reality of God can occur immediately. Whether new on the path or with much experience, it is helpful for all who aspire to illumination of consciousness to fervently yearn to soon awaken to their full potential and to maintain their unwavering conviction that it is possible.

No external power or intelligence can actively interfere with or prevent our spiritual growth. The redemptive influences of grace are not provided to some people and withheld from others. The effects of our past actions (karma) which influence our personal affairs relate only to mundane circumstances, not to our soul destiny. Intentional right living and attentive spiritual practice does not actually cause spiritual growth; constructive actions remove mental and physical restrictions that cloud the mind, allowing soul awakening and unfoldment to occur naturally.

Spiritual growth, whether slow, medium, or fast, is always in accord with one's responsiveness to the innate inclination to be spiritually awake, the actions performed to remove restricting influences, and the ability to accurately discern the difference between truth and untruth—between what is real and what is not.

Because we tend to habitually think about and identify our awareness with that which we deem important above all else, it is fairly easy to determine what we consider to be of most value to us. If we are preoccupied with matters which we say we wish we could avoid, or would like to have removed from our lives, why do we allow ourselves to be overly concerned about them? When desire to unfold and actualize spiritual potential is sincere only constructive thoughts are allowed to prevail in the mind; only wholesome personal relationships are acceptable; a healthy lifestyle is maintained; dedication to the fulfillment of meaningful purposes determines decisions; regular interludes of contemplative prayer and meditation practice are included in daily regimens.

Our present states of awareness, moods, modes of thinking, behaviors, relationships, and circumstances, whether influenced by subconscious tendencies, willed by our conscious intentions, or agreed to by us as they begin to express, are of our own choosing. By learning to clearly discern the difference between ourselves as spiritual beings and the disordered mental processes and fragmented states common to ordinary awareness, we can choose not to allow subliminal tendencies and debilitating habits to determine our circumstances. By assuming personal responsibility for the choices we make and the actions we perform, we can actualize psychological health and emotional maturity necessary for well-being and spiritual growth.

Rational thinking, constructive actions, and the cultivation of innate soul qualities effectively resist, restrain,
weaken, and eliminate problem-causing subconscious conditionings. Our awareness is then more easily expressed
through the mind and body and we are enabled to know
that we are spiritual beings only playing a human role in
the material realm. Our intellectual skills increase; our
powers of intuition are unveiled; our ego-sense is purified. We become increasingly cosmic conscious, enabled to
apprehend that highest and best knowledge: that all souls
and all things abide in God's wholeness.

The *truth* to be clearly apprehended and fully realized, rather than passively acknowledged, merely believed,
or professed as a creed, is that one Reality exists. The
Absolute, the transcendent aspect of Consciousness, is
without attributes or characteristics. Incomprehensible to
anyone who is mind-identified, that field of Existence-
Being is knowable when soul awareness is no longer confined by the limitations of the material medium of the
mind. The aspect of Consciousness (God, the Oversoul)
directly involved in the manifestation, preservation, and
dissolution of universes has attributes and characteristics that make possible its expressive influences. God produces the worlds by the emanations and interactions of
cosmic forces. Because the universe abides in the omnipresent field of God's being, God's presence pervades and
enlivens the universe and regulates its processes.

Souls, as individualized aspects of God's being, have
all of the attributes and characteristics of God. Because
souls are not other than God, they cannot have independent existence nor can they ever be separate from God.
The word used to define the true essence or reality of the

soul is *Self*—which is not to be confused with one's ego-centric, illusory, or presumed sense of personal selfhood. The Self, like God, is never seen; only its influences are objectively manifested. Accurate Self-perception and experience of our true nature is Self-realization. Accurate perception and experience of God is God-realization. Self-realization can be accomplished by contemplating the true nature of the Self. It can also be accomplished by meditating until awareness is removed from involvements with the senses and the mind, and by an act of grace—a sudden soul awakening to a transcendent state of awareness.

At the innermost level of our being we are Self-aware and have complete knowledge of God and of cosmic processes. When our surface awareness is clarified, this knowledge is reflected in it. Then, in the course of everyday living, our enlightenment persists.

Enlightenment is flawless realization of the totality of Consciousness. A momentary, partial enlightenment episode, while perhaps empowering, is not liberating. Unqualified freedom from delusions (erroneous beliefs or ideas) and illusions (errors of perception) is accomplished only when enlightenment is permanent.

There are various causes of physical birth of souls. Some become unconsciously involved with Nature's processes. Others incarnate because of their interest, curiosity, desires, or because conditions in this realm correspond to their prevailing mental states and states of consciousness. Regardless of the cause of one's physical birth, when awareness of the opportunity to awaken to higher understanding dawns, the primary aim should be to resolve the problems created by prior unenlightened thoughts or actions and quickly accomplish spiritual growth to the stage of Self- and God-realization.

The four requirements for effective and successful living and the fulfillment of spiritual destiny in this incarnation are:

- Knowledge that we are where we belong in the universe, doing what is best for our well-being and the well-being of others and the environment while living in harmony with Nature's laws and the processes of evolution.
- Knowledge and skills that enable us to live effectively and have our life-enhancing desires easily fulfilled.
- Affluence or prosperity: evident as a continuous, timely flow of resources, events, circumstances, and relationships appropriate to and supportive of our meaningful purposes in life and which amply provide for our needs.
- Authentic spiritual growth that culminates in Self- and God-realization and liberation of consciousness.

Every person who is capable of rational thinking is free to choose a life-path. A course of uncertain, imprudent, or purposeless actions will almost always result in confusion, misfortune, and despair. The way of clearly defined, constructive actions will definitely result in mental clarity, permanent good fortune, and rapid unfoldment of soul qualities and powers of perception.

My guru often said that right, concentrated practice of Kriya Yoga quickens spiritual evolution, enabling the devotee to realize, in one life cycle, perfected Self- and God-realization that might otherwise require several incarnations to accomplish.

To practice Kriya Yoga effectively and successfully, do these things:

- Maintain a wholesome, constructive, purposeful lifestyle.
- Be attentive to spiritual practices that will increase Self-awareness and awaken and unfold innate knowledge.
- Be initiated into advanced meditation practices and personally instructed in philosophical and practical matters by a spiritually awake, knowledgeable teacher-representative of this tradition who embodies its principles.
- Be fully committed to discipleship. A disciple (learner) diligently applies what is learned to remove or overcome mental and physical conditions that confine or restrict awareness; increase soul capacities and be receptive to grace; and purify the ego (the illusional sense of self-identity) to allow the full reality of God to be apprehended and realized.
- Meditate regularly to nurture overall well-being and to frequently experience superconsciousness (*samadhi*).

Because of their importance, these essential matters are more fully explained in the following chapters.

The real purpose for being born into this world
is much different than what most people imagine.
Life has a fundamental purpose. To know it, we
must understand where life comes from and where
it is going. We must consider its highest potential
for development and look beyond our immediate
goals to what we want to ultimately accomplish.
Paramahansa Yogananda

TWO

Lifestyle Guidelines

Because all who choose this path of light are advised to practice meditation, devotees may erroneously believe that, when a degree of proficiency in meditation practice is acquired, they are doing all that is necessary. For Kriya Yoga practice to be effective, we need to be attentive to all actions that enable the accomplishment of the four aims of life described in the first chapter. (1) Have a harmonious relationship with the universe and live with meaningful purpose. (2) Have knowledge and abilities that make possible the easy fulfillment of life-enhancing desires; (3) Constantly be in the flow of appropriate, supportive events and resources. (4) Experience progressive, authentic spiritual growth that culminates in Self- and God-realization and liberation of consciousness.

Now reminded of what is required of you—if you sincerely desire to live effectively and fulfill your spiritual destiny in this incarnation—fervently aspire to accomplish the highest and best of which you are capable. Be resolute in your commitment to live with conscious intention so that everything you do will be your spiritual practice. On this path, your thoughts must be rational. Your actions must be constructive, intentional, and purposeful. Delusional or illusional thinking must be renounced. Laziness, procrastination, and passive, ineffective actions should be replaced by enthusiasm for learning and living, timely and appropriate responsiveness, and soul-motivated result-producing actions.

To have a harmonious, supportive relationship with the universe, apprehend it as it is—an undivided, whole manifestation of interacting cosmic forces emanated by one Consciousness. The energy of the universe neither increases nor decreases; it is transformed from one state to another. Because you, as an individualized aspect of Consciousness abide in this field of wholeness, you can discover your relationship to it and have its support. To the extent that your awareness, thoughts, and actions are constructively coordinated, in like measure will events, relationships, and personal circumstances be expressed in your life.

- Nurture your relationship with God and with God's energies expressing as the universe by being constantly aware of the Presence of God, thinking and acting constructively, and living in accord with the laws of Nature.
- Pray for guidance.
- Meditatively contemplate your role in life. Inquire within yourself to discover what you are here to do with the knowledge and skills you now have or can acquire.
- What should you endeavor to accomplish?
- What service should you render to others and to society?
- How can you accomplish your constructive purposes?
- What you can do, or can envision as being possible for you, begin now to do.
- Think of your creative participation with the orderly processes of life as a great adventure: as a welcome opportunity to learn, expand your capacities, and unfold and express your innate qualities and powers.

- Organize your life. Establish your priorities. Decide what is important and what is not.
- Master your thinking, emotions, and behaviors. What you think, feel, or do that enhances your life and contributes to spiritual growth is acceptable. Avoid thoughts, feelings, and behaviors which contribute to mental or emotional unrest or cause problems of any kind.
- Choose a lifestyle that is fully supportive of your total well-being and your aspiration to spiritual growth.
- Wisely choose your friends and companions. Associate with people who share your aims in life and spiritual aspirations without being dependent upon them or becoming overly involved in nonessential matters.
- Relate to the world, but rely only on God and your ability to live effectively in accord with your growing understanding and your faith in the orderly processes of the universe.
- Be Self- (soul) centered rather than self- (ego) centered.

Egoism and egotism are the two obstacles to spiritual growth rooted in self-centeredness. *Egoism*, the illusional perception of "I-ness," causes feelings of being separated from God and of having weak or diminished capacities to learn and accomplish. *Egotism (arrogance*, an exaggerated sense of self-importance) is often dramatized as aggressive, selfish assertiveness. To overcome or avoid these problems, let your awareness expand rather than remain contracted. Renounce provincial (small or narrow-minded) attitudes and behaviors. Be willing to grow to emotional maturity. Acknowledge your responsibilities to yourself and to others. Attend to your spiritual practices. Let the quality of your life, enhanced by your awakened spiritual consciousness, silently influence collective human and planetary consciousness.

Express the soul qualities of patience, compassion, and appropriate adaptability in relationships and to circumstances. Renounce impatience, disinterest in the welfare of others, aversion to learning how to communicate effectively with others, and aversion to effective, functional living. Although the universe appears to be illusory when the causes of its manifestation are unknown, it is not an illusion. Inability to perceive the wholeness of Consciousness is the cause of our illusions. View the world as a manifestation of lights and shadows occurring in space-time.

Choose to be prosperous—to thrive, flourish, and be successful. You can then live comfortably, efficiently accomplish all of your meaningful purposes, and have abundant resources available to use for the general welfare and spiritual uplift of others who will be benefited by your compassionate acts. Cultivate a prosperity consciousness. Avoid thoughts and feelings of lack, limitation, or need. Renounce cravings, and tendencies to dominate, grasp at or cling to things, relationships, or circumstances. Assume and maintain an awareness of having what you want or need. You abide in the ocean of God's consciousness. Your mind is one with Cosmic Mind. Nothing separates you from God. The all-pervading, primordial substance of Nature is available to you in whatever form that may be required to provide for your needs.

At the innermost level of your being, you are ever serene and problem-free. It is only at surface levels of awareness that mental confusion and emotional unrest are dramatized. By self-training, learn to assume and maintain the mental states, emotional states, and clarity of awareness you deem to be most desirable and useful. By doing this, subconscious conditionings will be weakened and eliminated. Their forces will be transformed into creative energies you can productively use. Do not believe yourself to be a victim of outer circumstances, genetic characteristics, adverse planetary influences, or karmic conditions. The true Self cannot be touched by any external condition. All circumstances can be improved or changed. Genetic characteristics need not always be a controlling factor. Planetary influences are minimal and cannot adversely effect you when you are soul-centered and purposeful. Karmic conditions can be weakened, removed, or transcended.

If you are committed to the path of light, adhere to lifestyle regimens that conform to your commitment. Doing this will keep you soul-centered, improve your receptivity to the impulses of grace, and concentrate your attention on matters essential to your well-being and the accomplishment of your major purposes. Adapt the routine outlined at the end of this chapter to your personal circumstances.

Your body is nourished by soul force that flows into it through the medulla oblongata at the base of the brain, the food you eat, the water you drink, and the air and life force (*prana*) you breathe. Adhere to a wholesome, natural, vegetarian diet, high in fiber and nutrition-rich, in moderation and appropriate to your needs. Drink only pure water. Juices of fresh fruits and vegetables and herbal beverages can also be used. Energize your body and mind by right living, obtaining adequate sleep, exercise, and meditation practice.

Exercise should be adapted to your basic mind-body constitution (see *Ayurveda* in the Glossary). For a *vata* constitution, free-flowing, moderate exercise is most suitable; extremely fast, frantic, exercise should be avoided. For a *pitta* constitution, exercise should be moderate and noncompetitive. For a *kapha* constitution, exercise can be more strenuous and enduring. Walking, swimming, hatha yoga practice, and t'ai-chi are suitable for all constitutions. Chiropractic adjustments and other bodywork, as needed, can be helpful.

Healthy, long, physical life is of value because it makes possible the accomplishment of major purposes, including Self-realization, in one incarnation. Learn the philosophical principles and regimens of Ayurveda and use them to balance the subtle governing principles that influence your psychological and physical states.

Simplify your life. Avoid being unduly influenced by the erratic or restless behaviors of others or by news of current community or international events. Avoid excessive socializing and idle, meaningless conversations. Be moderate in sexual activities. Renounce worry, anxiety, fear, uncertainty, and all debilitating habits. Conserve your vital forces and use them for entirely constructive purposes. Wisely manage your money and other personal resources. Until you are established in Self-realization, frequently remind yourself that you are an immortal spiritual being abiding in the Infinite ocean of God's consciousness. Actualize your highest potential for growth and expression in accord with your understanding.

Monitor your thoughts and how you live your life:

- Are you sincere about being Self-realized in the years that yet remain for you in this realm?
- Do you sometimes think that conditions will be better in the astral realm after you depart this world, or in

the next incarnation?

- Are you hoping that a saint or guru will intercede on your behalf to assure your salvation?
- Are you passively accepting circumstances which are neither satisfying nor fulfilling?
- Are you clinging to a belief system or letting your mind be confused by illusions?
- Are you passively allowing yourself to be at the mercy of unwholesome habits and addictive behaviors?
- Are you in control of your thoughts and emotions?
- Do you study truth literature?
- Do you meditate regularly and correctly?
- What are you doing to assist yourself to your highest good?
- Are you really doing your best to learn, grow, and unfold your innate capacities to apprehend the reality of God?

I am not the guru. God is the guru. I am only God's servant.
Paramahansa Yogananda

Restless flows of prana (life force) cause mental
restlessness. When the truth seeker is established
in superconsciousness, meditation practice is
natural and spontaneous. Then, even when one
is not meditating, its benefits are enjoyed.
Lahiri Mahasaya

A Recommended Daily Routine
for Devotees on the Path of Light

- Awaken early in the morning. Acknowledge your relationship with God. Pray and meditate. Read a selection from the Yoga-Sutras, the Bhagavad Gita, or words of truth from other inspired writings.

- Established in meditative calmness, turn your attention to your schedule of activities for the day.

- Perform your duties cheerfully, skillfully, and with alert attention. Purposeful, intentional, effective living is as important as meditation practice. Remember that every person, creature, and thing has a spiritual essence. Relate to and nurture it.

- Have your meals on a regular schedule. Exercise daily. Before concluding the day's activities, mentally plan your work or activity schedule for the next day. Live in the moment, look to the future.

- In the afternoon or evening, meditate for a few minutes to reduce stress, refresh the mind and body, and maintain your attunement with the Infinite.

- Go to bed early. Sleep in God.

THREE

Spiritual Practices

The philosophical principles upon which the teachings of this path of light are based can only be completely known when they have been diligently applied, tested, and verified by personal experience. The word origin of *diligent* is Latin *diligens*, from *diligere*—to choose, esteem, or love; characterized by persevering endeavor. Correct, attentive, persistent practice of the constructive actions described in this chapter will:

- Enable you to focus your attention on your major purposes, empower you with enthusiasm, and sustain the momentum that will keep you on your chosen life-path.
- Weaken and eliminate subconscious influences that may otherwise fragment and blur your awareness.
- Awaken dormant soul forces and allow them to flow freely.
- Facilitate orderly, rational thinking.
- Purify the intellect and improve powers of discernment.
- Purify the ego, allowing Self-awareness to prevail.
- Restore awareness to its natural, clear state, allowing Self- and God-realization to more easily be experienced.

Remain aware of why you are practicing. Avoid being so preoccupied with procedures and techniques that you forget their purposes; they are only the means to the accomplishment of desired outcomes. The results of right spiritual practice are clear awareness, orderly, spontaneous thinking, and intuition-directed actions which are always appropriate to needs or circumstances. In the second chapter of the Yoga-Sutras, the fundamental practices of Kriya Yoga are described:

- The virtues of harmlessness, truthfulness, and honesty are to be demonstrated by thoughts, words, and behaviors.
- Vital forces are to be conserved and constructively used.
- Mental and emotional attachments and addictive behaviors are to be renounced.
- Psychological health is to be nurtured and maintained by calm self-analysis; pacifying and neutralizing subconscious conditionings which cause discomfort or distort awareness; resolving mental confusion and emotional conflicts; eliminating addictive tendencies; replacing self-defeating behaviors and mental attitudes with constructive behaviors and attitudes; renunciation of delusions and illusions; regular, attentive meditation practice.
- Physical cleanliness and good health are to be maintained.
- Soul-contentment in all circumstances is to be nurtured.
- Intellectual and intuitive analysis of Consciousness—the reality of one's true nature and of God—is to be continued until Self-knowledge and God-realization are perfected.
- Ego-consciousness, the illusional sense of selfhood, is to be diminished and purified to allow the primary, innate urge to be awake in God to prevail.
- Meditation is to be practiced on a regular schedule.

For many sincere truth seekers, a major obstacle to spiritual growth is that, although they know they are not the personality-self, and yearn to be Self- and God-realized, the illusional sense of being separate from God persists.

Disinterested in ordinary circumstances, unable or unwilling to renounce erroneous notions or traditional ways of thinking, their awareness is clouded and conflicted by subliminal influences. They may tend to allow feelings of despair to prevail over aspiration to enlightenment, and inclinations to be apathetic to inhibit energetic, constructive actions. They may withdraw into a mind-created realm of fantasy and illusion, hoping for improvement to occur in the near or distant future.

Confused, ego-fixated devotees often superficially examine various philosophical systems or obsessively engage in a variety of private rituals or practices. They may seek out and attempt to learn from several teachers or participate in group endeavors which have a "spiritual" orientation. In these, and other ways, they continue to look outside of themselves for knowledge that is within them and for God in which they already abide. A common, unwise, choice is that of continuing to live a normal, self-conscious life with the support of companions who are also frustrated and unhappy.

The ordinary human conscious condition is like a painful disease for which the cure is known, but is not always easy to acknowledge or apply. Most people will admit to sometimes feeling lonely, unfulfilled, insecure, and fearful. Memories of past errors of judgment or behavior may cause feelings of remorse and sadness. Memories and feelings of trauma experienced during occasions of misfortune or mistreatment may be vivid and psychologically debilitating. Knowledge of the inevitability of physical death may cause thoughts and feelings of hopelessness and helplessness to hover like a dark cloud. It may then be difficult to believe that happiness, health, affluence, functional freedom, mental illumination, and spiritual enlightened is attainable.

Right spiritual practice supported by insightful, wholesome, constructive, purposeful living is the infallible cure for all of the suffering, difficulties, and incidents of misfortune that are related to the ordinary human conscious condition. Most people whose awareness is dim and confused live their lives in a semiconscious, dreamlike state, with sequential episodes and events having little or no real meaning or value. Because of their habitual behaviors and the compelling influences of karmic conditions, they repeatedly experience similar circumstances.

The path of light is enjoyable because liberating. To be Self- and God-realized, we only have to discern the fact of our true nature as it is, and apprehend and experience the reality of God as the one, eternally existing wholeness in which we are included.

Every day, resolve to meditate more deeply
than you did the day before. Focus your attention
within. You will experience new power, strength,
and peace of body, mind, and spirit. All bonds that
presently limit you will be vanquished.
Paramahansa Yogananda

Without Self-knowledge, there is no possibility
of having true peace. When one's attention is allowed
to dwell on objects of desire and the senses become
stimulated, the mind follows, as a boat on the water
is carried away by the wind. Mental restlessness
then obscures Self-knowledge.
Sri Yukteswar

FOUR

Initiation and Discipleship

Initiation is a "new beginning," a significant event that contributes to a radical reorientation of viewpoint, restores the disciple's awareness to a soul-centered state, and almost always causes beneficial changes in lifestyle and behavior. The rite of initiation may be a ceremonial event accompanied by ritual or it may be informal. The great essential is that it be empowering. Even if several individuals are instructed in philosophical principles and basic practices during the occasion, initiation is always given directly by the guru to the disciple.

In the Kriya Yoga tradition, initiation is offered by a guru or by a disciple-representative of a guru who has been given permission to initiate others. A teacher who presents information of any kind can rightly be referred to as a guru. A *satguru* (*sat*, is-ness, truth, the reality of being) is a teacher who imparts life-transforming knowledge by word and example, transmits the spiritual force of consciousness, and assists the disciple to experience psychological changes and spiritual growth. A satguru's primary role is to encourage disciples to purify their ego, improve their powers of intellectual discernment, and rapidly accomplish spiritual liberation.

In this Kriya Yoga tradition, one who requests initiation into this path of light must:

32

- Be sincere (dedicated, honest, and unpretentious).
- Have respect for the tradition and for the teacher.
- Be willing to learn and to practice what is learned.
- Have the intellectual capacity to learn and the functional ability to apply what is learned.
- Adhere to a constructive lifestyle and engage in regular, meaningful spiritual practice.
- Prepare for initiation by thoughtfully contemplating the responsibilities of discipleship.
- During and after the rite of initiation, be attentive to and abide by the teacher's instructions in regard to lifestyle, behavior, and spiritual practices.
- Study the philosophical principles upon which right living and spiritual practices are based, be firmly resolved to quickly awaken to Self-knowledge and God-realization, and demonstrate their resolve by appropriate actions.

When we are not soul-centered, our attention tends to flow outward, involving our awareness with mental states, moods, sense perceptions, and mundane circumstances. Thus extroverted and with awareness fragmented, we may become forgetful of our spiritual essence and life's wholeness, and be inclined to compliantly conform our lives to ordinary modes of behavior. Awareness can be restored to wholeness by: (1) withdrawing attention from externals and directing it inward so that Self-awareness is maintained and thoughts, moods, and sense-perceived circumstances can be viewed with objectivity; (2) commitment to spiritual awakening and growth; (3) participation in processes that remove mental and physical obstacles to spiritual growth.

When initiating a prepared devotee, the guru:

- Explains fundamental philosophical principles and describes

the lifestyle regimens to be implemented.
- Provides instructions for meditation practice.
- Explains the use of meditation techniques.
- Requests that the new initiate, now a disciple, affirm his or her commitment to the tradition and to faithfully practice what has been taught.
- As an authorized representative of the lineage of gurus, blesses the disciple and transmits the spiritual force of consciousness—acts which make initiation meaningful.

Mantras and words of instruction given at the time of initiation are considered to have their own potency. They are also infused with the special quality of creative force imparted to them by the guru's consciousness and intention, and the vibrational frequency of the spiritual force that flows through the guru. The subtle connection that is established between the disciple's mind and consciousness and the vibrational force that flows through the guru is to be nurtured and strengthened. When this connection—the basis of the guru-disciple relationship—is maintained, it keeps the disciple's mind and being attuned and receptive to supportive, redemptive mental and spiritual impulses flowing from the guru and the lineage of gurus. The consciousness of a God-realized guru is, in fact, a conduit through which transformative, soul-enlivening grace can express.

In this Kriya Yoga tradition, disciples are taught the following meditation techniques:

- A meditation mantra, because it is easy to learn and practice. When proficiency in meditation practice has been acquired, initiation is offered.
- When initiation is given, three techniques are taught. (1) A

procedure for awakening vital forces in the lower chakras. (2) *Kriya pranayama*, by which life force is directed through the spinal pathway and brain. (3) A technique used to contemplate light in the spiritual eye and listen to the Om vibration. When the disciple's skills are improved and indications of psychological and spiritual growth are evident, advanced meditation techniques may be taught.

The new meditator is instructed to practice kriya pranayama fourteen times each morning and evening and meditate for a while in tranquil silence. The technique used for contemplation of inner light and sound is then practiced. After several months, as advised by the teacher, the number of pranayama repetitions can gradually be increased. By correct, regular practice of this technique, physical relaxation is elicited, mental processes are calmed, the nervous system is refined, subliminal tendencies that cause mental and emotional transformations are pacified, meditative concentration is improved, and superconscious states are more easily experienced.

When psychological and physiological health is good and lifestyle and environmental conditions are ideal, in the normal course of evolution the human brain is progressively refined and spiritual growth occurs naturally. One complete cycle of kriya pranayama practice, during which a current of life force is directed upwards and downwards through the spine, is believed to have the same enlivening and regenerative effect on the brain and nervous system as does one solar year of constructive living supported by ideal lifestyle and environmental conditions. Because regular, correct practice of Kriya Yoga meditation techniques refines the nervous system, elicits superconscious states, and allows soul awareness to more easily express through the mind and body, the devotee's spiritual growth is accelerated.

These methods cannot be effectively learned from books, nor is secondhand transmission of information of real value. If it is not convenient to be initiated by one's guru, it is acceptable for a qualified, initiated disciple of the guru to perform the initiation and be available for personal counsel.

To avoid confusion and to remain focused on the spiritual path, disciples of this tradition are asked not to discuss these techniques with others, and to refrain from talking about their personal practices and meditative experiences. The disciple's attention, energies, and actions should be directed to purposeful living, study, and contemplative meditation. The years go by quickly; one should nurture awareness of the Presence of God and be attentive to practices that can make possible spiritual enlightenment. Service should be rendered in accord with one's means and capacity while remaining soul-centered, with thoughts and actions devoted to the heart's desire to be fully awake in God.

Neither spiritual instruction nor initiation can be purchased from a guru. At the time of initiation, one may make a modest donation to be used for charitable purposes. Disciples may also volunteer their services or contribute financially to support the guru's teaching mission so that other truth seekers may be benefited.

An enlightened guru never manipulates or abuses disciples or selfishly attempts to control their thoughts or actions. Disciples are encouraged to use their own powers of discriminative intelligence, intuition, and common sense, and to wisely exercise freedom of choice. Although gurus provide practical advice and endeavor to attune themselves to the mind and consciousness of receptive disciples for the purpose of transmitting their inner realization, they should not be thought of as magicians to whom one might go, or pray to, with expectations of having personal problems instantly solved or miracles performed on their behalf. The guru is a spiritual friend whose primary role is to assist disciples to be Self-realized.

Attunement with one's guru and the lineage of gurus can be nurtured by maintaining unwavering faith in the value of the relationship; being respectful; living constructively; meditating regularly; and practice of constant awareness of the Presence of God.

Because the guru's enlightened consciousness is not influenced by the conditioned states of others, when the relationship between a guru and a disciple is close because of physical proximity or because of mental and spiritual attunement, the disciple's opinions and attachments to habitual modes of behavior are likely to be challenged. When this occurs, a wise disciple will choose be receptive and responsive to spiritual growth opportunities.

These teachings should not be diluted by endeavors to adapt them to incompatible philosophical concepts. When you are certain that you are on the right path, respect enlightened teachers of all traditions and the paths that others have chosen, while adhering to the way which you know to be best for you. This Kriya Yoga path emphasizes essential matters common to all enlightenment teachings.

Because of sincere aspiration to spiritual growth, and attunement with the guru, the disciple's latent spiritual force (*kundalini*) may be awakened. The effects of this awakening may either be mild or dynamic in intensity. They produce psychological transformations and cause adjustments of states of consciousness which enable one to practice meditation more easily and effectively. There is nothing to fear in regard to kundalini awakening; it is your own creative power.

The vital forces of spiritually unawake people flow mostly downward, identifying their attention with the body, mind, and sense perceptions. When spiritual awakening occurs, vital forces flow upward, regenerating and refining the body and mind and somewhat detaching attention from mental states and the senses. Awareness is then clarified, superconscious states are more easily experienced, and spiritual growth effortlessly occurs.

Some devotees experience mental confusion and emotional unrest because their desire to accomplish mundane purposes diminishes and activities and relationships which were formerly considered by them to be important are no longer of interest. Although ego-identification is somewhat weakened, soul awareness and innate knowledge may not yet be sufficiently unfolded to enable wise choices and decisive actions. If this condition occurs, view it as merely a temporary stage of transition.

When your path in life is not yet known, refuse to be mentally or emotionally depressed or to succumb to feelings of loneliness, despair, or apathy. Be quietly enthusiastic, energetic, and purposeful. Choose your moods, states of consciousness, and actions. If this is not done, your thought processes, moods, states of consciousness, and behaviors may be influenced by subliminal tendencies, habits, and external conditions. Nurture your inner strength. Improve your intellectual and intuitive powers.

Perform all duties cheerfully and skillfully. Maintain a daily routine of metaphysical study and spiritual practice. Be happy. Let your soul serenity emerge and prevail.

Be soul-content and patient. Nurture devotion to God. Think of yourself as an agent for highest good in the world. It is not necessary to feel that you have a great mission to fulfill; your primary purpose in this incarnation is to be awake to the truth of your being and your relationship with the Infinite.

Anticipate and be thankful for the good fortune and spiritual growth that unfolds. Right living provides opportunities to experience fulfillment; anxiety about the future or expectations of being rewarded for actions invites disappointment. You are now abiding, and will ever abide, in eternity. Learn to do it well.

When seeking guidance, endeavoring to solve problems, or meditating, do not rely on "voices" or visions; they are only products of your mind. Avoid involvements with individuals who claim to be agents through which messages from enlightened teachers are conveyed; they are either deluded or dishonest. Enlightened souls never communicate through mediums.

Devotees whose intuitive powers are developed may, when meditating, occasionally perceive what appears to be the likeness of saintly beings or of other people who are either embodied or deceased. Although authentic telepathic and clairvoyant communication with saints and ordinary people is possible, it is rare. Visions and other phenomena which may be experienced when meditating are usually wish-fulfilling mental creations. Devotees on this path are advised to awaken to superconscious realizations which transcend such perceptions.

When the devotee's awareness is no longer distorted by subliminal influences, delusions, or illusions, the only remaining obstacle to Self-realization is egoism: the soul's identification with thoughts and feelings of independent selfhood. When ego-sense is purified, knowledge of the soul as an individualized aspect of the one Consciousness is acquired. When the purified ego is transcended during superconscious meditation, or at other times, realization of oneness prevails.

The guru's duty is to direct the disciple's attention to that which is real. The disciple's duty is to listen, observe, study, learn, and faithfully practice what is learned until soul liberation is accomplished.

Give Kriya [instruction and initiation] to all
who humbly ask you for help.
Mahavatar Babaji, to Lahiri Mahasaya

If you pray with devotion, the magnetism
of your devotional ardor will attract God's
presence into your awareness.
Paramahansa Yogananda

FIVE

Meditation Routines

The practitioner of yoga should steadily contemplate the Supreme Reality, in solitude, alone, with mind and body controlled, having no cravings for anything. In a clean, suitable place, established in a firm meditation posture, there, intent upon practice, with thoughts and senses subdued, let the devotee practice meditation to purify the mind. With body and head erect, motionless, gazing into the spiritual eye with focused attention, serene, fearless, established in a vow of self-control, concentrating on that Supreme Reality, one should steadfastly sit, devoted to the highest realization.

– The Bhagavad Gita 6:10-14

Meditation should be practiced daily. The easiest way to ensure regularity of practice is to meditate early in the morning after a night of restful sleep, before thinking about the day's duties and projects. If this not possible, schedule your practice when you can do it, and adhere to that schedule. When your meditation routine is established, you will joyfully anticipate the opportunity to abide in the sanctuary of silence.

Fifteen to twenty minute meditation sessions will clarify awareness, calm and organize mental processes, reduce stress, refine the nervous system, strengthen the immune system, slow biologic aging processes, and enliven the organs, glands, and systems of the body. When meditating for the purpose of experiencing refined superconscious states, sit longer.

If you have been initiated, allow as much time as necessary to practice the meditation techniques. After practicing a meditation technique, rest in the tranquil silence. Remain alert. Avoid passive sitting with thoughts and moods dominating your awareness or with your attention preoccupied with personal problems, projects, or fantasies. The easiest way to meditate is to listen to a mantra, a pleasant word or word-phrase that will attract your attention and keep it focused.

Sit comfortably, poised and upright, with your spine erect. Inhale more deeply than usual. Exhale. Do this two or three times. Relax. Be still. With your eyes closed, look into the spiritual eye center. Be aware of your natural breathing rhythm. Mentally recite the mantra with inhalation and exhalation.

The word "God" may be used as a mantra. Mentally recite it when you exhale. As your body becomes relaxed, and thoughts and emotions are quieted, breathing will be slower and thoughts and moods will be less distracting. When your attention is internalized, mentally "think" or "listen" to the mantra rather than recite it. If your attention wanders, bring it back to the mantra. When your mind is quiet, disregard the mantra and rest in the peaceful silence for the duration of the practice session. If thoughts, moods, memories, or random mental images interfere with concentration, or if you are too passive and only semiconscious, resume the use of the mantra until you are again alert and meditation flows smoothly.

The purpose of meditation practice is to calm subconscious impulses which cause thoughts and mental transformations to occur. Preliminary superconscious perceptions are usually mixed with subtle thoughts and shifting moods. When awareness is clear and concentration is steady, superconsciousness devoid of thoughts and emotions will be experienced. When using your mantra, there may be an occasional, brief pause in your breathing pattern that occurs after exhalation. Notice during the momentary pause, that thoughts are more subtle, and sometimes cease. At such moments, notice how you feel when your awareness is clear. With practice, you can assume a state of clear, thought-free awareness at will.

When using a word-phrase mantra, mentally recite, or "listen" to the first word with inhalation and to the second word with exhalation. Remember to allow inhalation and exhalation to occur naturally. There is no need to attempt to regulate the process. The Sanskrit mantras, *so-ham* (so-hum), *ham-sa* (hum-sa), or *hong sau* (hong-saw) are easy to use and their vibratory potency has a calming effect on the mind. If your guru has given you a mantra, use it. Otherwise, use one which appeals to you. Use the same mantra each time you meditate.

Even when the difference between self-awareness and the mind and physical body can easily be discerned, awareness may yet be egocentric: contracted and confined by the erroneous notion of independent existence. What is needed is a shift of viewpoint that results in experience—along with knowledge—of your true nature. Then Self- and God-realization can be accomplished.

When meditating, if you perceive light at the spiritual eye, let your attention be attracted to it. The light that is seen manifests because certain brain centers are being stimulated. Subtle sounds may be heard in the inner chambers of your ears. Let your attention be attracted to them. If you hear a steady, flowing sound, consider it to be an aspect of the Om vibration. Merge your awareness into it, remembering that God is its source. Expand your awareness in Om to reclaim your awareness of wholeness. The reality of God is where you are. Acknowledge, apprehend, and experience that reality when you meditate. Remain Self-aware and God-conscious after you meditate.

When meditating, being aware of inner light and sound can keep your attention internalized. If what you perceive or experience changes, it is not the reality of being, the absolute wholeness you aspire to realize. With gentle intention, extend your awareness beyond all transitory perceptions and experiences.

Avoid anxiety about the results of meditation practice. Perform the right actions and appropriate results will naturally unfold. The following routine can be accomplished in twenty to thirty minutes. For superior results, practice once or twice a day on a regular schedule:

- In a quiet environment, sit upright. With your eyes open, look straight ahead for a few moments until you are poised and relaxed. Then close your eyes. Direct your attention to (and be aware at) the spiritual eye center between and above the eyebrows.
- Begin meditation practice with prayer. Pray only to attune your awareness with the Infinite.
- If meditation flows spontaneously, let the process occur.
- If a technique is needed to elicit physical relaxation and calm the mind, listen to your mantra until your attention is internalized. When your thoughts and emotions are settled and your awareness is tranquil, disregard the technique. Rest in

the silence. Remain alert. Have no anxiety about the outcome. Consider regular, attentive meditation practice to be your spiritual duty.

- Let your sense of personal selfhood fade and dissolve. Be aware of wholeness. Rest in conscious, tranquil awareness of wholeness until you are inclined to conclude the session.
- After meditation practice, be mentally peaceful, emotionally calm, Self-aware, patient, and God-attuned while attending to your ordinary duties.

If you perform simple exercises or practice Hatha Yoga prior to meditating, experiment to discover whether it is more helpful for you to do this before or after you meditate. Some devotees report that physical activity prior to meditation makes it difficult for them to quiet the mind. Others say that their mild exercise routine has a relaxing effect, enabling them to meditate more effectively. Do what works best for you.

If you are a Kriya Yoga initiate, use the techniques and meditation practice routines exactly as prescribed by your guru. Use your mantra anytime, to unstress the nervous system and calm the mind. It can also be used at the beginning of a longer meditation session, or later when you are aware of the need to remove your attention from thoughts and emotional states or to refocus your attention when you become too passive.

If you meditate daily for thirty minutes to an hour, schedule a longer session once a week, twice a month, or once a month.

Remember that living a balanced, purposeful life is just as important as metaphysical study and meditation practice. The functional and intellectual abilities and the powers of concentration that you acquire as the result of intentional, skillful living will enable you to more easily comprehend the reality of Consciousness and to meditate effectively. Your clarified awareness and the exceptional powers of perception that will unfold as the result of your spiritual practice will enable you to live more creatively and enjoyably.

The sages declare that the most enlightened
devotees are they who, having realized that objects
of the material world are, in reality, Consciousness,
are not disturbed by the sorrows that accompany
the cycles of birth and death.
Sri Yukteswar

By deep meditation and living for God alone, calm
the waves of thought and desire that modify your
perception of reality. Then in superconsciousness
you will behold everything as it really is.
Paramahansa Yogananda

Meditation is [spontaneously] experienced when we are
aware of the presence of God within us. God is revealed
within when our awareness is made pure by liberating
it from all concepts of duality and finitude.
Lahiri Mahasaya

Part Two

The Yoga-Sutras

Introduction to the Yoga-Sutras

Sutras (Sanskrit verb-root *siv*, to sew) are concise "threads" of teaching concepts of a designated theme which are to be meditatively contemplated until intellectual and intuitive apprehension of their meaning prevails in the truth seeker's awareness. The exact date of the composition of the original Sanskrit text of the *Yoga-Sutras*, attributed to the philosopher seer Patanjali, is not known: some scholars estimate it to be at least two thousand years ago.

In the first chapter, samadhi (superconscious) states are explained and various ways to accomplish them are mentioned. Kriya Yoga procedures are described in the second chapter. In the third chapter, *siddhis* (exceptional abilities) are defined, with emphasis on the importance of their being primarily used to remove obstacles to spiritual growth. The means by which soul capacities may be actualized and the signs which indicate the final stages of soul awakening prior to and including liberation of consciousness are presented in the fourth and final chapter.

Read all four chapters to acquire an overview. Then, when in a quiet, meditative state, start with chapter one and read a verse, or a few verses on a given theme. Contemplate the meaning of what you read. If possible, do this on a daily schedule.

For some of the sutras, brief supplemental notes are included to more fully explain their meaning.

ONE

Samadhi, and the Means of Accomplishment

1. Now, instruction in yoga [samadhi] in accord with an established tradition, begins.

The word *now* is used to indicate that the guru is qualified to teach the disciplined procedures (the means) by which *yoga* (superconsciousness) may be accomplished and has the authority to do so. The word is also used to acknowledge that the student is prepared to learn and to practice. The occasion is thus *auspicious* (favorable): a timely moment when the disciple can experience a *transition* to a higher stage of growth.

In this text, the word *yoga* means samadhi: superconscious awareness which is other than and superior to ordinary states of awareness. Ordinary states of awareness are blurred and fragmented because of the prevailing influences of gross or subtle mental modifications.

Reference to an *established tradition* indicates that what is being taught is not new or original. It is universally applicable because it is a continuation of the transmission of knowledge that has been known, tested, and verified by others.

2. Yoga [samadhi] is realized when fluctuations in the individualized field of awareness cease because of having been restrained and returned to their origins.

This sutra (*yogah chitta vritti nirodha*) describes the precise means of success in practice. *Yogah* (samadhi is) accomplished when the *vrittis* (fluctuations) in *chitta* (the individualized field of awareness) are restored to their inactive, dormant state by the practice of *nirodha* (restraining and turning back).

3. When fluctuations in awareness cease, the seer [the perceiver, the true Self] abides in its own nature.
4. When not abiding in its own nature, the seer is inclined to identify with the fluctuations and their modifying influences which manifest in the field of individualized awareness.

Because our true nature is pure consciousness, when our awareness is clarified, the essence of our being is experienced. When our attention is not established in awareness of pure being, it is inclined to flow to and identify with mental and emotional states which are influenced and modified by subliminal impulses, memories, and sense perceptions.

5. Modifications of awareness are fivefold [and of two kinds]. They may be afflicted, painful, impure, and imbued with restricting influences; or not afflicted, not painful, pure, and devoid of restricting influences.

Modifications are changes or limitations imposed on mind-identified soul awareness. Afflicted modifications are the result of lack of Self-knowledge, egoism (inaccurate Self-identity), fascination with and attraction to externals and non-essentials, aversion to that which is disliked or may cause pain or discomfort, and fear of death and after-death states. They cause discomfort and disrupt flows of attention and creative forces. Modifications of awareness which are not afflicted allow attention and creative forces to flow freely.

6. The five modifications of individualized awareness are valid knowledge, misperceptions [illusions], fantasy [and hallucination], sleep, and memory.
7. The three means of acquiring valid knowledge are direct perception, inference, and the testimony of others who are knowledgeable.

Valid (true, verifiable by application) knowledge can be acquired by direct perception, observation of the facts which support it, and by learning from others who are already knowledgeable.

8. Illusions are inaccurate perceptions.

When we only presume to know the facts about what we observe, our illusions can result in irrational thinking and unwise behaviors. The primary illusion of the undiscerning soul is that it is independent of the one Consciousness, God.

9. Fantasy is imaginary cognition unsupported by an existing object of perception.

Illusions are related to objects (things or circumstances) which are inaccurately perceived; fantasies, being entirely mind-originated, have no external cause or support. Ordinary fantasies are unregulated imaginal creations, like waking dreams enacted in the mind. Excessive indulgence in fantasy may be an endeavor to avoid having to confront reality. When fantasy is allowed to be habitual, or occurs because of biochemical imbalance, stress, sleep deprivation, or other causes, hallucinations may manifest and be mistakenly believed to have objective reality.

10. Sleep is a modification of the power of cognition supported by Self-observation.

Ordinary sleep is a semiconscious state characterized by internalized attention and corresponding physiological changes. We are never completely unconscious. Upon awakening, we remember whether or not the interval during which we slept was satisfying. As our awareness is clarified by intentional living and spiritual practices, we sleep more consciously, and dreams, during which the mind organizes information, are more luminous and orderly. Eventually, restful, superconscious sleep similar to a deep meditative state can be experienced.

11. Memories are mental images of prior perceptions.

Whatever is observed, sensed, experienced as an emotion, or thought about, is impressed in the subconscious level of the mind as a memory (Sanskrit *samskara*). Memories enable us to relate past events to present circumstances and provide a sense of history. Memories which are afflicted because of being associated with recollections of trauma or misfortune may cause feelings of distress. Even memories of pleasant events, if excessively dwelt upon, can be obstacles to purposeful, effective living. Preoccupation with memories of all kinds can result in the accumulation of new memories (of related thoughts and feelings that are generated), thus increasingly modifying awareness and obscuring the soul's ability to perceive clearly.

12. Fluctuations and modifications in the individualized field of awareness can be restrained, restricted, and removed by meditation practice and dispassionate non-attachment.

Thoughts and moods that blur awareness and distract

attention should be regulated and subdued. Attention is concentrated and directed inward during meditation practice. When involved in ordinary activities, calm, objective observation of thoughts, moods, and circumstances pacifies thought processes and elicits emotional calmness.

13. Of these two [practices], attentive concentration on a chosen object or ideal is meditation.
14. Meditation practice becomes firm and steady by persistent, devoted endeavor.

Regular, alert meditation practice removes attention from distractions and directs it to the chosen object or ideal to be known or experienced. Persistent, devoted practice results in superconscious realizations that provide actual experience of the difference between clear states of awareness and ordinary modified or conditioned states.

15. Dispassionate nonattachment is accomplished by renouncing cravings and instinctual urges.

Cravings (persistent desires) and instinctual urges which are grounded in the mind and body and do not originate in the soul, are easily renounced by observing them with an attitude of calm detachment.

16. The most accomplished renunciation results from Self-realization which enables one to disregard and transcend the actions of the cosmic forces regulated by the constituent attributes of Nature.

Three constituent *attributes of Nature* (*gunas*) regulate the actions of cosmic forces. The attribute of *Sattva guna* is evident in orderliness, brightness, and illumination of consciousness.

Rajas guna is evident in movement and transformation. *Tamas guna* causes inertia and dullness. These three influences can also be observed within our mind and body. Our thoughts and moods can be elevated, constantly changing, or dull and sluggish. We can feel physically light and free, restless and aggressive, or heavy and apathetic. To live effectively and experience rapid unfoldment of soul qualities, it is recommended that *sattvic* (elevating) characteristics be cultivated; *rajasic* (transformative) characteristics be disciplined and directed to higher purposes; and *tamasic* (heavy, awareness-clouding) characteristics be overcome and avoided. To do this, thoughts, moods, actions, personal behaviors, relationships, and foods should be selectively chosen as determined by common sense, intellectual discernment, and one's aspiration to actualize total well-being, mental illumination, and liberation of consciousness.

17. The samadhi of wisdom is accompanied by gross and subtle thoughts, ecstatic tranquility, [partial] Self-realization, and the joyful experience of oneness with universal consciousness.

The *samadhi of wisdom* is a preliminary stage during which various perceptions are present, including those of thought processes which are either strongly evident or extremely subtle in intensity and character. Even though this superconscious state may be accompanied by unusual and enjoyable perceptions, it is tainted by the presence of awareness-modifying characteristics and the influences of the attributes of Nature. Although it provides some insight, it is not liberating. It can be encouraging because it provides perceptions of possibilities yet to be realized. It should not, however, be considered as a final attainment nor be allowed to result in attachments to fleeting perceptions of a subtle character.

18. The other samadhi leaves a residue of impressions in the mind.

The *other samadhi*, realized when fluctuations in the meditator's field of awareness cease, is transcendent. It leaves a memory-impression (*samskara*) in the mind which, because of its superior character, weakens and displaces troublesome mental impressions made in the course of ordinary, self-conscious living.

19. Samadhi without complete knowledge may be temporary. From this state, one may continue to higher realizations or again become involved with the gross realm and the actions of Nature.

If Self-realization is not complete, even though external objects of perceptions are not observed one may still be involved with analysis of primary Nature and its influential characteristics. From this level, the characteristics of primary Nature may be transcended or one may again become involved with its aspects. The outcome is determined by the devotee's state of consciousness and where attention is directed.

20. The other samadhi is preceded by Self-awareness, disciplined endeavor, enthusiasm, attentive meditation, and the awakening and emergence of wisdom.

The *other* [pure] *samadhi* that results in liberation of consciousness is realized by right endeavor, persistent, repeated practice of superconscious meditation, and spontaneous Self-unfoldments of knowledge.

21. For those whose practice is intensive and whose progress is fast, samadhi is near.

22. For those who aspire to samadhi, progress is in accord with their endeavors; whether they are mild, medium, or extremely intentional.
23. Samadhi can be realized quickly by surrendering [self-consciousness] to [in] God.

Egoism, the illusional sense of independent selfhood, is the major obstacle to Self- and God-realization. When ego-sense is purified, the illusion of separateness ceases.

24. God is not restricted by Nature or karma.

God, the aspect of the one Consciousness which emanates universes and regulates their processes, is neither limited by the characteristics or actions of Nature nor influenced by causative influences (karma) and their effects which occur in the relative realms.

25. God is omniscient, omnipotent, and omnipresent.
26. God, transcending time, space, and karma, is the true guru, the teacher of even the ancient teachers.

An embodied guru (teacher) can communicate information about God and cosmic processes, explain how to live effectively, and provide guidelines for spiritual practice. Soul-liberating knowledge, being innate to the soul, is revealed from within. Embodied teachers are only representatives of the Truth; God alone is the true guru.

27. The evidential aspect of God is Om.

The sound-vibration emanated from God's consciousness is described as Om (the Word). Its presence is evidence of the existence of its origin.

28. Meditation on Om culminates in knowledge of its meaning and in Self- and God-realization.

When the meditator's attention is internalized and awareness is withdrawn from the mind and senses, subtle sounds can be heard. When preliminary sound-frequencies are replaced by the steady-flowing sound of Om, Om can be listened to and merged with while contemplating the one Consciousness, the source from which it originates.

29. By attentive practice of meditation on God, God is realized and all obstacles are removed.
30. [Some] obstacles to accomplishment of samadhi are illness, doubt, negligence, philosophical confusion, failure to make progress, instability, addiction to pleasurable sense perceptions, misperceptions, and mental distractions.

When we are God-realized, our awareness is clarified and difficulties related to conditioned states of consciousness cease to exist. Until we are God-realized, to the extent of which we are capable all conditions and circumstances which obstruct spiritual growth should be minimized or eliminated by attentive personal endeavor. To heal or to avoid illness, regimens which contribute to vital health should be chosen and implemented. Doubt can be replaced by faith. The habit of negligence can be overcome by adopting constructive mental attitudes and personal behaviors. Philosophical confusion can be eliminated by acquiring accurate information about God, the soul, Nature's processes, and how to nurture the unfoldment of innate soul qualities. Progress in spiritual growth can be experienced by living constructively and by skillful meditation practice. Mental and emotional instability can be replaced by cultivating mental peace, self-confidence, and emotional maturity. Addictions of all kinds can be renounced by resolute choice and by concentrating on practices that facilitate rapid spiritual growth. Mental distractions can be eliminated by living with intention, improving powers of concentration, prayer, and regular, sustained practice of superconscious meditation.

31. [Some] symptoms of mental distractions are grief, anxiety, unsteadiness of the body, and irregular breathing.
32. To master and eliminate these distractions, one should meditate on a real object [such as Om or any aspect of God].
33. The individualized field of awareness is calmed and purified by the cultivation of ideas [and feelings] of friendship, compassion, joy, and dispassion, and by contemplating possibilities of accomplishments yet to be actualized.
34. Or one may definitely overcome all such obstacles by practice of pranayama.

Pranayama is practiced by regulating the processes of inhalation and exhalation to encourage life forces to flow freely. Pranayama occurs naturally when life forces are unobstructed. Pranayama practice should be learned from a qualified teacher.

35. Perception of subtle cosmic forces and their actions and manifestations causes changes in the meditator's awareness which contribute to mental stability.

When we are aware of subtle processes occurring in our field of awareness, we can experience constructive adjustments of mental states and states of awareness by choosing to identify with elevating influences.

36. Changes which contribute to mental stability also occur because of the natural, clear and luminous [*sattvic*] mental state that prevails.
37. By emulating and actualizing the virtues and states of consciousness of role models and saints, the devotee's awareness becomes calm and harmonized.

By assuming the mental states, states of awareness, and modes of behavior of others who are knowledgeable and skillfully functional, we can experience the benefits of those constructive states and actions.

38. One's awareness can also be clarified by acquiring knowledge of dreams and of dreamless sleep.

When we are aware of our natural, pure conscious state, ordinary waking states and sleep states can be known as modifications of the mind which need not be allowed to interfere with our continuous and permanent Self-awareness.

39. One's field of awareness is also clarified by alert meditation on a chosen object of attention that is pleasing or agreeable.

When sitting to meditate, if the object to which attention is directed is attractive, concentration will be effortless. In the early stages of practice, a mantra may be used to focus attention and elicit physical relaxation and mental calmness. When mental processes are somewhat subdued and attention is internalized, one may meditate on inner light, Om, or any aspect of God, or gently aspire to Self-knowledge and realization of pure consciousness.

40. By practicing meditative contemplation one can acquire mastery of matter, from its minute aspects to the greatest magnitude.
41. When awareness is clarified, it accurately reflects whatever is presented to it.
42. When, because mental transformations persist, the devotee's awareness is not tranquil, insightful perceptions, random thoughts, and illusions are intermingled.

Clear perceptions, streams of thoughts, and illusory ideas are mixed during preliminary superconscious states. Distractions can sometimes be minimized or avoided by choosing to ignore them. They can definitely be eliminated by cultivating mental and emotional calmness and merging awareness in Om and pure consciousness.

43. When samadhi without mental transformations is steady, the meditator's awareness reflects the reality of pure consciousness.
44. By this knowledge, samadhi mixed with thought processes and samadhi devoid of thoughts and mental transformations are understood.
45. Samadhi modified by subtle influences of the gunas and their qualities continues until awareness is removed from identification with the field of primary Nature.

Even when the mind is calm and superconscious states are easily experienced, the devotee's awareness may still be somewhat influenced by the three attributes of Nature. *Tamasic* influences may partially obscure the meditator's perceptions and incline the devotee to be attached to pleasurable perceptions. *Rajasic* influences may contribute to astral perceptions and ecstatic states which, while interesting and perhaps enjoyable, keep the devotee's attention bound to phenomena. *Sattvic* influences are illuminating.

46. Preliminary states of samadhi are supported by mental transformations.
47. When awareness is clarified, the reality of the true Self is revealed.
48. Direct perception of Truth is then realized.
49. Knowledge acquired by having conversations, reading books, ordinary modes of learning, and preliminary samadhi states differs from intuitive knowledge.

Acquired knowledge is useful information. Intuitively perceived knowledge is direct perception of what is true.

50. Mental impressions made by the samadhi of wisdom inhibit, weaken, transform, and dissolve other mental impressions and produce permanent, beneficial changes.

The superior influences of superconscious states illumine the mind, weaken addictive tendencies, dissolve mental impressions, clarify awareness, and allow Self-determined behaviors. The spiritually free state that results enables the devotee to live without karmic compulsion while continuing to awaken to complete Self- and God-realization.

51. After gross mental impressions are dissolved, the constructive mental impressions of samadhi states also dissolve. God-realization then prevails.

With mind and ego purified, the fully enlightened soul is liberated from all that formerly restricted its awareness.

TWO

Kriya Yoga

1. Austerity, study, and surrender to God are the means to the accomplishment of perfect concentration. These practices comprise the path of Kriya Yoga.

Austerity—disciplined regulation and mastery of sensory and mental impulses, adjustment of mental attitude, and behavior modification—results in psychological transformation that frees soul awareness from addictive attachments and erroneous notions that confine it.

Study includes insightful analysis of one's true nature and of Consciousness and its categories and aspects.

Surrender to God is accomplished by cultivating devotion that merges the practitioner's awareness with the one Consciousness and by renouncing the illusional sense of independent selfhood.

Kriyas are "actions" performed to nurture psychological and physical health and spiritual growth. The result of attentive practice is *yoga* (samadhi): the reunion of soul awareness with the wholeness of Consciousness.

2. Kriya Yoga is practiced to weaken and remove all obstacles that interfere with the accomplishment of the samadhi of God-realization.

3. The restricting influences which contribute to pain and suffering and interfere with God-realization are egoism, illusions, attachments, aversions, and confusion

about the processes of birth and death.

4. Imperfect perception of the real nature of Consciousness is the primary cause of all restricting influences, whether dormant, weak, aroused, or uninterrupted in their actions.

Flawless apprehension of the reality of Consciousness is only possible when we are Self-realized. Until we are fully awake to Truth, it can be helpful to use intelligence and intuition to discern the difference between our awareness and the various mind-body states which are observed. It will be apparent that the one who observes is not that which is observed. We then know "I am neither the body nor the mind." So long as we are identified with the body and the mind, our awareness is inclined to be influenced by mental and physical states. Our constructive actions and practices do not cause spiritual growth; spiritual growth occurs spontaneously when restrictions are weakened or removed by our actions or the influences of super-conscious states. Even when engaged in practices to eliminate mental and physical obstacles to the free flow of awareness, it is important to remain established in Self-identity.

5. Ignorance of what is true causes one to erroneously presume the noneternal to be eternal, the impure to be pure, the painful to be pleasurable, and the ego to be the real Self.

6. Egoism results from identification of the soul's awareness with mind and gross matter.

Without knowledge of the origins of the universe, the soul presumes the realm of Nature to be permanent; ordinary circumstances to be ideal and satisfying; and conditioned, self-conscious awareness to be the real state of being. The truth is just the opposite: universes are emanated and dissolved; ordinary circumstances are temporary; the sense of independent selfhood is illusional.

7. Preoccupation with pleasurable sensations and objects of pleasure produces affection for them that causes attachments.

8. Being repulsed by that which causes discomfort or pain produces aversion.

Pleasurable sensations need not restrict the free flow of soul awareness. Fascination with and strong *attachment* to pleasurable sensations and circumstances, and to behaviors which are instrumental in producing them, fixates, confines, and contracts soul awareness.

Aversion to that which is known (or is believed) to cause pain or discomfort is a normal self-preservation reaction. When identified with personality characteristics and ordinary circumstances and relationships, egocentric souls may have feelings of aversion in regard to learning the facts of life and to engaging in spiritual growth practices that would definitely change their perception of themselves and their relationships.

9. The urge toward death [non-being], along with the urge to live, propelled by instinctive drives, is deeply rooted even in the wise.

The urge toward non-being is caused by *tamasic* influences which blur awareness and incline it to be unconscious. For spiritually unawake souls, the urge to live may be impelling because of fear of death along with strong attachment to the personality-self identity and to existing circumstances. For souls aspiring to spiritual growth, the urge to live is nurtured by the innate inclination to be forever awake and knowledgeable.

10. Subtle restricting influences can be overcome by resolving them into their origins.
11. Gross restricting influences can be eliminated by superconscious meditation practice and awakened knowledge.

If restrictions (egoism, illusions, attachments, aversions, confusion about the processes of birth and death, and karmic conditions) which contribute to pain and suffering and interfere with God-realization are only mildly influential, they can be overcome by right Self-identification, rational thinking, renunciation, appropriate behaviors, and acquiring accurate information about the soul's sojourn in time and space. If the influences of any or all of these restrictions are pronounced, they can be weakened and eliminated by regular, sustained practice of meditation.

12. An accumulation of karma rooted in the primary restriction may cause corresponding effects in this or other life cycles.

The *primary restriction*, the cause of all problems and misfortune because it blurs awareness and distorts perception, is the delusion (erroneous notion) that one is other than an immortal spiritual being already abiding in the unbounded field of God's consciousness.

13. As long as causes exist, their effects may manifest and contribute to either pleasure or pain.
14. Pleasure or pain, or joy or sorrow, can result from the effects of destructive or constructive subjective causes.
15. Because of the existence of latent mental impressions yet to be influential and the actions of the constituent

attributes and cosmic forces in Nature, the possibility of pain exists even in the midst of pleasurable circumstances.

Some subliminal mental impressions (karmic conditions) manifest circumstances which are immediately perceived as being restrictive or painful. Other subjective causes manifest events and circumstances which afford temporary pleasure but eventually culminate in pain and misfortune. Enjoyable circumstances produced by constructive subjective causes can restrict spiritual growth if mental and emotional attachments to them are allowed to occur or if circumstances are determined only by karmic influences. When good fortune is experienced, its causative influences may weaken and become impotent. Latent karmic impressions may become activated. Boredom and purposelessness may contribute to apathy. Unwise living habits may unbalance the mind-body constitution. A disturbance of the influences of the gunas may cause psychological unrest and physical distress. The certainty of eventual physical demise may be painful to contemplate.

16. Pain and suffering which has not yet been experienced is to be avoided.
17. Suffering is due to the soul's excessive identification with the mind and body and their processes.

Subjective causes with potential to manifest events, and circumstances which may be painful or limiting, can be weakened and eliminated by applying the practices described in this treatise. The immediate way to avoid future suffering and misfortune is to awaken to Self-knowledge which eliminates the primary awareness-restricting habits of ego-fixation and delusional identification with mental and physical conditions. When one is enlightened, perceptions are accurate, behaviors are wisely chosen, and the supportive, redemptive actions of grace can prevail.

18. The objective realms, composed of elements, powers of sensation, thought, and action, and influenced by the constituent attributes of Nature, serve the purpose of providing Consciousness with the means for expression and liberation.

A creative force, emanated from God, manifests the realm of primordial Nature (Om and its self-expressed aspects of space, time, and cosmic forces). From the realm of primordial Nature, the universe is objectively manifested. All aspects of Nature provide Consciousness with the means for expression.

19. The [three] constituent attributes of Nature have four aspects in accord with their gross or subtle expressions: the specialized, the unspecialized, the indicated, and that which is devoid of characteristics.

The sixteen *specialized* aspects are earth, water, fire, air, and ether (cosmic matter in space); five sensory organs; five organs of action; and the mind.

The six *unspecialized* aspects are the five subtle states of the specialized manifestations which precede their expression, plus egoism.

The *indicated* aspect, known by its presence, is the faculty which makes possible intellectual determination, by which the mind-identified soul can acquire knowledge.

The fine aspects of cosmic forces which are *devoid of characteristics* reside in the primary field of Nature and make possible the manifestation of the universe.

20. The Self, while observing that which is present to be perceived, remains pure consciousness.

Just as God is not confined by the cosmos or limited by the actions which occur in it, so we need not be confined or limited by that which we observe. When we are established in Self-realization, memories, thoughts, feelings, and objective phenomena can be observed and appropriately related to without any blurring or fragmentation of our awareness.

21. The purpose [of the existence] of the universe is to provide Consciousness a field for expression.

The universe, produced by impulses from God's being, persists as a field in which God's consciousness and aspects are expressive until the cosmos is withdrawn into the realm of subjective, primordial Nature. After a duration of dormancy during which the constituent attributes of primordial Nature are in a state of equilibrium, another universe is emanated. Souls which are not liberated prior to the dissolution of a universe become involved with the newly manifested universe to continue their experiences and spiritual growth.

22. Although the universe is no longer observed by the Self which has transcended it, it continues to be perceived by souls which are in relationship to it.

23. Cosmic forces emanated from the field of God mix with the field of primary Nature, causing soul awareness to be identified with it.

24. Imperfect awareness of its true nature is the cause of the soul's identification with mind and matter.

25. When the soul's delusion of being identified with matter is removed, ignorance ceases and absolute freedom is experienced.

God's Spirit (Life) shining on the field of primordial Nature is reflected as individualized aspects of pure consciousness— the true essence or Self of every person and creature. Individualized aspects of pure consciousness which assume an illusional sense of independent selfhood (egoism) and become identified with mental and physical characteristics are referred to as souls. Liberation of consciousness occurs when the awareness of the Self is removed from tenacious identification with mental and physical characteristics, the three attributes of Nature, and cosmic forces.

26. Unwavering intuitive knowledge of God is the means by which suffering caused by delusion is eliminated.
27. For the insightful devotee, the elimination of restrictions to Self-realization may be experienced in seven successive stages.

During the *first stage* of awakening, one discerns the obstacles which have to be removed if further unfoldment is to be experienced. This insight makes possible wise, concentrated, constructive endeavor.

The *second stage* is accomplished when restrictions with the potential to cause pain or misfortune have been neutralized to the extent that they cannot cause pain or misfortune in the future.

The *third stage* is accomplished when superconscious states which make possible the examination of fine levels of consciousness are frequently experienced.

The *fourth stage* is accomplished when the meditator clearly comprehends the relationship of the soul to the mind and to internal and external phenomena.

At the *fifth stage*, impressions in the mental field no longer contribute to changes in the soul's field of awareness.

The *sixth stage* is God-realization. Cosmic forces cease to be influential in causing changes in the soul's awareness.

At the *seventh stage*, the soul, free from all physical and mental restrictions and influences of Nature, permanently abides in conscious realization of pure being.

28. By the practice of the disciplines of yoga, restricting influences are weakened and clarification of awareness to the stage of discriminative discernment [enlightenment] is accomplished.

Knowledgeable, skillful practice results in purification of awareness that allows direct perception of what is real.

29. Refraining from destructive behaviors, actualizing constructive behaviors, a steady meditation posture, regulation and transformation of vital forces, internalization of attention, concentration, meditation, and samadhi are the eight stages of practice which enable the devotee to accomplish God-realization and liberation of consciousness.

By actualizing the eight stages of practice, the devotee experiences psychological and physical health, orderly relationships, and the full support of Nature. Karma accumulated because of previous actions is dissolved; subliminal impulses are pacified; awareness is clarified; realization of wholeness is complete and permanent.

30. The five restraints to be perfected are avoidance of doing harm, untruthfulness, theft, dissipation of vital forces, and covetousness.

31. They are universal because their application is not limited by time or cultural circumstances.

Regardless of the era in which one lives or the cultural circumstances which prevail, devotees who aspire to liberation of consciousness are advised to be steadfastly committed to perfecting these fundamental practices.

32. The five constructive behaviors to be observed and perfected are cleanliness, contentment, mastery of mental and sensory impulses, study and analysis of Consciousness, and surrender to God.
33. To neutralize and overcome destructive instinctual forces, the opposite forces should be cultivated by choosing and performing constructive actions.
34. Subliminal and instinctual drives and tendencies may be mild, moderate, or strong. Because they may cause pain and suffering, they should be removed by the performance of virtuous actions.

Destructive drives and tendencies which may cause thoughts and feelings and incite actions which are harmful to oneself or to others are rooted in ignorance. Weakening and replacing them by cultivating constructive thinking, nurturing emotional maturity, and performing life-enhancing behaviors is the best way to quicken psychological transformation that clarifies awareness and allows spiritual growth.

35. In the presence of a person who is established in harmlessness, all living things are devoid of enmity.

Enmity (ill will, animosity) cannot coexist with the field of compassionate acceptance radiated by one who has perfected the virtue of harmlessness.

36. When one is established in truthfulness, immediate results of actions occur.

Accurate perception eliminates mental and emotional confusion and allows skillful actions to produce intended results.
Actions performed may include the intentional assumption of
states of consciousness and mental and emotional states, and
the implementation of thoughts, will, and behaviors for the
accomplishment of purposes. Whatever a person who is established in Truth-consciousness affirms to be true can be believed.
Whatever such a person says will occur in the near or distant
future is certain to manifest. A Truth-conscious person can, by
gentle intention, inclination, or acceptance of envisioned outcomes, cause desires (their own or those of others) to be easily
fulfilled and needs to be spontaneously met.

37. One who is established in non-stealing experiences
    permanent affluence.

When a state of "enlightened desirelessness" prevails, the
reality of one undivided, all-pervading Consciousness can be
apprehended. When clear awareness of the Self-sufficiency of
wholeness is unwavering, affluence—a continuous, uninterrupted flow of supportive events, relationships, and resources—
is spontaneously experienced.

38. By conservation and transmutation of vital forces,
    abundant energy is acquired.

Vital forces are diluted and wasted by stress, worry, preoccupation with memories and fantasies, restlessness, purposeless or misdirected actions, excessive eating, eating foods or
using substances which are difficult to assimilate or which poi-
son the body, excessive talking, insufficient sleep, and other
behaviors which are not life-enhancing. Devotees on this path
of light are advised to consider everything they do as spiritual
practice. Right living results in effective performance of duties,

orderly and supportive circumstances, well-being, clarity of awareness, and rapid unfoldment of innate qualities. Conserved life force is transmuted into a finer aspect of vital force (*ojas shakti*) that energizes mental powers, strengthens the body's immune system, enlivens the nervous system, transforms the brain, and empowers one to accomplish meaningful purposes.

39. When cravings to possess unnecessary things are renounced, one acquires the ability to know the processes of birth and death [of beginning and ending of events that occur in time and space].

Nonattachment allows awareness to expand to cosmic consciousness, thus enabling one to intuitively know the relationships between causes and their probable effects.

40. Because of physical cleanliness, one enjoys good health and immunity from sources of contagion.
41. From the purity of the *sattvic* attribute of the mind arise serenity and cheerfulness, improved powers of concentration, victory over the senses, and fitness for direct perception of God.
42. Contentment [that prevails in all circumstances] bestows supreme peace and happiness.
43. Perfection of the body, mind, and senses results from self-disciplined acts of purification.
44. By [insightful] study and [right] spiritual practice, direct perception of the reality of God [and the categories and processes of Nature] is realized.
45. By the cultivation of intense devotion and surrender [of the illusional sense of selfhood], realization of God is perfected.

Unwavering soul contentment in all circumstances can be nurtured by being established in Self-awareness while dispassionately observing one's thoughts, feelings, and behaviors, the behaviors of others, and the emergence and disappearance of events and circumstances.

46. A stable, comfortable, and pleasant sitting posture is ideal for the practice of meditation.
47. When deep relaxation is accomplished and mental transformations cease, awareness is released into the field of infinite Consciousness.
48. When restrictions [to concentration] are removed and awareness is freed from involvement with the senses and mental transformations, uninterrupted unfoldment of superconscious states can occur.
49. Pranayama occurs naturally when the meditation posture is stable, breathing rhythms are coordinated and refined, and flows of vital forces are harmonized.
50. Modifications of pranayama are either external, internal, or motionless. They are long, short, or restrained, and modified according to space, time, and number.

When attention is internalized and life force flows freely, meditation occurs spontaneously. During the early stages of meditation practice, breathing may be externalized, internalized, or temporarily motionless because of an occasional pause. Inhalation and exhalation may be deep (long), shallow (short), or inhibited, or forceful, subtle, fast, or slow. Heavy, forceful breathing confines awareness to the senses. As stress is reduced and physical relaxation occurs, breathing becomes slow and subtle, and mental and emotional states are calmed.

51. A fourth modification of pranayama is that of neutralizing the inflowing and outflowing breaths.

When the two aspects of life force (*prana* and *apana*) which
are influential during inhalation and exhalation are neutralized, meditation can be effectively practiced. Practice of Kriya
Yoga pranayama neutralizes these aspects of life force.

52. Mastery of pranayama removes the darkness that veils
the light [self-luminous reality] of the soul.
53. By pranayama practice, mental processes are ordered
and clarified, freeing attention to be concentrated on
God.

The darkness that obscures the soul's perception of its true
nature is lack of Self-knowledge, which may be reinforced by
restless or conflicted mental processes and *tamasic* influences
present in the mind and body. When pranayama (life force flowing freely) occurs naturally or is nurtured by intentional practice, *sattvic* influences become pronounced, *rajasic* influences
that cause mental transformations are neutralized, and aware-
ness-blurring characteristics of *tamasic* influences are weakened and removed.

54. [When meditating], internalization is accomplished
by withdrawing awareness and vital forces from
externals and directing them inward to their source.
55. By internalizing awareness, supreme mastery of the
senses is acquired.

When awareness is involved with mental processes and the
senses, meditation cannot be successfully practiced. When the
body is relaxed and the mind is somewhat calmed, awareness

and life forces can be directed inward to the spinal pathway, then to the spiritual eye and higher brain centers. Detaching attention and awareness from the senses and from desire for sensory stimulation is the most effective way to accomplish Self-mastery of the senses and of subliminal impulses.

THREE

The Unfoldment of Soul Abilities

1. An unwavering flow of attention is concentration.
2. Concentration directed to an object one aspires to know or an ideal to be realized is meditation.
3. The self-shining of the object of meditation devoid of obstructing characteristics is samadhi.
4. Concentration, meditation, and samadhi, practiced together, is meditative contemplation.
5. Mastery of meditative contemplation results in the emergence of illuminating, intuitive knowledge.
6. Intuitive knowledge should be applied to discover progressively higher levels of consciousness.

Devotees who aspire to Self-realization should know what they are endeavoring to accomplish when they meditate. Concentration results in meditation; steady meditative contemplation results in samadhi—either identification of awareness with the object of meditation (samadhi with support) or the free state of wholeness (samadhi without a supporting object). Awakened intuitive knowledge and unfolded abilities should be applied to accomplish pure or transcendent samadhi. Intuition and abilities used primarily to accomplish mundane purposes further restrict awareness and limit the soul.

7. The three practices [concentration, meditation, and contemplation] are internal in comparison to the five practices which precede them.

8. They become external when the samadhi which has no supporting object is realized.

The *five practices* which precede the practice of concentration, meditation, and meditative contemplation are the restraints and intentional actions described in chapter two (sutra 30 and 32), posture, pranayama, and internalization of attention. When samadhi without the support of an object of meditation is permanently realized, no further clarification of awareness is necessary. Meditative practices which preceded that realization are discontinued.

9. The superior, constructive influences of samadhi eliminate restrictive subliminal tendencies and instinctual driving forces.
10. The tranquil flow of awareness that then occurs is due to its innate purity.
11. Because of the influences of samadhi, fluctuations of mental modifications cease and awareness of wholeness prevails.
12. When the meditator's concentration is completely focused, sequential ideas that arise in the mind are similar.
13. The preceding four verses explain the kinds, fine variations, and states of transformations that occur in the meditator's field of awareness.

Sustained superconscious states weaken, subdue, and remove subconscious conditionings and the urges of instinctual tendencies. Awareness then flows naturally as impelled by its innate inclination. When practicing meditation prior to experiencing samadhi, ideas that arise in the mind are consecutive and similar rather than random and disconnected.

14. A substance has properties which have latent, not yet manifested, and expressive potentiality.
15. The orders and arrangements of subliminal impressions are the causes of their manifestations.

The mind is a substance because it is a manifestation of cosmic forces. A mind which is not yet fully illumined is conditioned by many impressions (*samskaras*) which have been accumulated as the result of the soul's mundane experiences and perceptions. These impressions comprise karma (subliminal influences with potentiality to cause effects) which may be expressed and thus neutralized; resisted, understood, and overcome; or transcended. How these mental conditionings are organized and interrelated determines how they may be influential. Devotees on the path of light are advised to (1) stop accumulating karma by living wisely and selflessly; (2) weaken the influences of subconscious influences by active resistance, mastery of sensory and mental impulses, and constructive thinking and behavior; (3) cultivate samadhi states by regular practice of superconscious meditation.

Note: In the following sutras, some results of successful practice of meditative contemplation are described. For these specific purposes, meditation is practiced until the mind is calm and awareness is tranquil. Attention is then directed to that which one aspires to know or experience until knowledge unfolds or the desired circumstance is actualized.

16. By contemplation on the threefold transformations of consciousness, knowledge of past and future can be acquired.

The *threefold transformations of consciousness* occur at the levels of unconsciousness (and subconsciousness), the ordinary conscious or waking state which is influenced by subliminal tendencies, and superconsciousness. The first two levels are ego- and mind-identified; all superconscious states indicate degrees of increased Self-awareness. Past events and experiences can be remembered. Future events and circumstances can be known by insightful analysis of their existing causes: the prevailing states of consciousness, mental attitudes, beliefs, expectations, desires, tendencies, and habitual behaviors. Undesirable, future events and circumstances of all kinds can be avoided by eliminating or changing their existing causes.

17. Words, their meanings, and ideas about them are often intermingled and confused. By contemplation on the words spoken by people and the sounds vocalized by creatures, their meanings can be comprehended.

The intentions, mental states, and states of consciousness of others can be known by observing their spoken words and discerning the purpose for their utterance. With practice, even the vocalized sounds of creatures can be interpreted with accuracy.

18. By contemplation on the influential forces of mental impressions [accumulated karma], knowledge of previous incarnations is acquired.

Because of the persistence of mental impressions, our present inclinations and desires may provide clues that can enable us to know how we lived and behaved prior to being born into this world. Although it is possible for some souls to remember events and circumstances that were perceived or experienced in previous physical embodiments and during sojourns in astral realms between physical incarnations, devotees who aspire to enlightenment are advised to avoid preoccupation with such matters. Clear memories related to past incarnations that spontaneously arise in the mind and provide helpful insight can be welcomed. Most endeavors to remember past incarnations culminate in purposeless speculation, illusory thinking, and excessive indulgence in fantasy—conditions in opposition to those which are supportive of spiritual awakening and the fulfillment of our destiny.

19. Meditative contemplation on the ideas presented by another person provides knowledge of the contents of their mind and states of awareness.
20. However, this apprehension of knowledge does not support the mental states or states of awareness of others because the purpose of knowing is not that of fully identifying with those states.

Ideas expressed or defined by another person can provide us with insight into how their mind processes information, the contents of their mind, and their habitual mental states and states of awareness. Our dispassionate observation does not result in complete identification of our thoughts or awareness with theirs.

21. By contemplation on the relationship of one's body and its light in relationship to the eyes of others, one can become invisible.
22. By this, the disappearance of sound, taste, touch, smell, and hearing is explained.

Because a material object which is not perceived by means of the senses is not observed, to be "invisible" one has only to decide to be unobserved.

23. By contemplation on karmic influences which are fast

or slow in producing effects, knowledge of events regarding [the circumstances of physical] death and other unusual occurrences can be acquired.

When subconscious conditionings are allowed to influence modes of thinking and behavior, their potency causes effects which correspond to their characteristics. When the driving forces of karmic influences are known, ordinary and unusual events that will occur in the near and distant future can be predicted with a reasonable degree of accuracy. Most spiritually unawake souls are fated to experience successive manifestations of circumstances produced by subjective causes until the potency of their karma is exhausted. Devotees who aspire to be removed from karmic influences can acquire knowledge of how to do so and diligently apply it. Subconscious conditionings can then be resisted by Self-disciplined actions and their potency transformed and directed to higher purposes. As spiritual awareness increases, karmic conditions become less influential. The soul's future circumstances are then determined by choice and by the impulses of grace.

24. Mental, moral, and spiritual strength is acquired by contemplation on friendliness, compassion, and other noble qualities.
25. By contemplation on various aspects of power, one becomes empowered.

Hostility, indifference, cruelty, selfishness, fear, refusal to acknowledge the innate divinity of others, and doubt are ignoble qualities. Friendliness, compassion, kindness, generosity, courage, willingness to acknowledge the innate divinity of every person, and faith in God are noble qualities to be nurtured and actualized. Although identification of awareness with various aspects of God's expressive forces is possible, the most soul-satisfying contemplative practice is that which results in Self-and God-realization.

26. By contemplation on the light of consciousness, intuitive knowledge of veiled, subtle, and remote things is acquired.

When the luminous reality of consciousness is apprehended, all of its categories and aspects, from the field of Existence-Being to the realm of gross matter, can be intuitively discerned.

27. By contemplation on the Sun [and its relationship to its planets and other phenomena in space], intuitive knowledge of planetary movements in space and of the evolution, persistence, and dissolution of the universe can be acquired.
28. By contemplation on the Moon and star systems, intuitive knowledge of their relationships and movements can be acquired.
29. By contemplation on the Pole Star, knowledge of the movements and relationships of the stars is acquired.
30. Contemplation on the chakra opposite the navel enables one to have knowledge of the body's systems.

The physical body through which our awareness flows and expresses is composed of cells grouped together to form tissues, organs, and the specialized circulatory, respiratory, digestive, excretory, endocrine, muscular, skeletal, and nervous systems. The organizing processes of the body are influenced by three governing principles (see *Ayurveda* in the Glossary).

31. Contemplation on the appetite and thirst centers provides mastery over hunger and thirst.

Although a moderate diet composed of nutrition-rich foods in accord with one's basic mind-body constitution is recommended and an adequate amount of pure water is necessary, compulsive ingestion of unnecessary foods and liquids should be avoided. With practice, the appetite and thirst centers can be regulated. Also, by nurturing awareness of the medulla oblongata at the base of the brain and the cervical chakra opposite the throat, and by remembering that the body is primarily vitalized by flows of life force that flow into it through the medulla oblongata, dependence upon gross food can be diminished. By using a little known technique, some yogis can vitalize the body with life force and live without food.

32. By contemplation on the center of equilibrium, stability of awareness is acquired.

The Sanskrit term *kurma-nadi* used in the original text is translated here as "center of equilibrium." *Kurma* means tortoise or turtle. A *nadi* is a channel through which life force flows. Meditative contemplation on the designated nadi will result in "turtle-like" slowness of respiration and calm, unwavering awareness. Experimentation will enable one to become aware of a current of life force flowing from the base of the brain downwards to the dorsal chakra. Identification with it results in unwavering, soul-centered awareness.

33. By contemplation on the light of the crown chakra, liberated souls have direct perception of Reality.

When awareness is clarified and restricting influences are absent, the soul is liberated and direct perception of the reality of God is constant. This sutra is sometimes translated as: "By contemplation on the light of the crown chakra, *siddhas* (perfected or liberated souls) may be perceived with inner vision."

Although it is the testimony of many saints that such perceptions are possible, the highest realization to which one should aspire is that of complete awakening in God.

34. By contemplation on absolute pure Consciousness, all innate knowledge is certainly revealed.
35. By contemplation on the heart [the reality of Being], knowledge of it is realized.
36. By contemplation on the self-existent reality of consciousness, one acquires the ability to clearly discern the difference between it and ordinary states of awareness and relative experiences.

Meditative contemplation on the supreme reality of pure Consciousness is the direct way to Self- and God-realization. The *heart* that energizes the mind and enlivens the body, and which is to be contemplated and realized, is the reality of Being. The true Self of us is ever pure and changeless; ordinary states of awareness are blurred and fragmented by fluctuations and transformations caused by restlessness and subliminal influences. When subliminal influences no longer prevail—because of having been subdued or transcended—alert Self-awareness allows the difference between it and conditioned states of awareness to be clearly discerned.

37. Because of meditative contemplation on the reality of God, supernormal powers of perception unfold.
38. If allowed to flow outward, these powers of perception become obstacles to further spiritual growth and to perfecting samadhi. If used wisely, they become superior abilities to be used to resist, weaken, and eliminate subliminal and instinctual influences which restrict free flows of awareness.

If extraordinary powers of intuition, hearing, touch, vision, taste, and touch are used only to fulfill mundane desires or to nurture egocentric inclinations, they interfere with spiritual growth. *Siddhis* (the powers or abilities that may accompany spiritual awakening) should be used to accomplish Self- and God-realization.

39. By removing the cause of attachment to the body and by focused concentration, one's awareness can penetrate the mind and body of others.

The *cause of attachment to the body* is the erroneous idea that one *is* a body, reinforced by sentimental attachment to mental, emotional, and physical states, and environmental conditions and circumstances. When a spiritual teacher's awareness *penetrates* the mind and body of a disciple, the teacher's Truth-realization and vital force is transmitted to the disciple in accord with the disciple's attunement and receptivity.

40. By mastering the upward-flowing aspect of life force in the body, one can be invulnerable to the various forces of Nature and consciously depart the body at the time of transition from it.

When the influence of the upward-flowing aspect of prana (*udana prana*) prevails, a feeling of physical lightness is sensed, one's awareness is identified with the higher chakras, and superconscious states are easy to maintain. The involuntary actions of this aspect of life force are regulated from the medulla oblongata and can be consciously regulated from the cerebrum. At the time of transition from the body, the upward flowing aspect of life force assists the soul's departure. If, because of an accident or illness, the transition process begins to occur prematurely, it can be delayed by an act of will.

41. When the actions of the vital forces of the lumbar chakra are free-flowing, inner and outer radiance [health and vitality] is manifested.
42. By meditative contemplation on Om, subtle sound perceptions are heard.

Preliminary sounds that are heard are the emanations of prana frequencies from the chakras. When a clear, flowing sound is heard, awareness can be merged with it while contemplating its source: the omnipresent field of Consciousness.

43. By contemplation on the relationship between the body and space, and identifying awareness with the idea of weightlessness, levitation is experienced.

While levitation of the body is possible, it should not be of primary interest to one who aspires to enlightenment. Of greater value is to acquire the ability to "elevate" one's awareness: to remove it from mundane influences which interfere with awakening to, and maintaining, Self- and God-realization.

44. By meditative contemplation on transcendent states beyond the gross modifications of the mind, the coverings that confine the Self are unveiled.
45. By meditative contemplation on gross matter, its essential attributes and components and their subtle aspects and drives, mastery over the energies and forces of matter is acquired.
46. By mastery of the elements, exceptional abilities become pronounced, the body and mind are refined and purified, and the indestructible qualities [the constituent attributes] of matter are known.

One *covering that confines the Self* is the primary delusion caused by imperfect Self- and God-knowledge. When, by intellectual discrimination and intuitive perception the nature of Consciousness (and its categories, aspects, properties, and processes) is known, one can live in harmony with natural laws and have their full support.

47. [Some] characteristics of physical perfection are attractiveness, bright complexion, strength, and adamantine hardness.

The word *adamantine* (having the hardness and luster of a diamond) is used to describe a healthy body vitalized by soul forces and impervious to disease because of its strong immune system.

48. By contemplation on the senses, their powers of cognition, inherent characteristics, pervasiveness and influences, mastery of them is acquired.

The senses receive information; perception of information allows it to be processed by the mind and interpreted by the intellect. Distinct from the senses, mind, and intellect, is the observing soul which is superior to them.

49. Having mastered the senses, and knowing the distinction between the attributes of Nature and the Self, supremacy over all states of consciousness is demonstrated.

50. By meditative contemplation on the distinction between the attributes of Nature and the reality of the one Consciousness, perceptions of omnipotence and omniscience are acquired.

51. When the causes of bondage have been removed by renouncing attachments to supernormal abilities and to perceptions of omnipotence and omniscience, soul awareness is restored to wholeness.

When individualized awareness is no longer confined, the soul's ability to apprehend the unrestricted power and complete knowledge innate to consciousness is reclaimed. Attachment to exceptional abilities and purified powers of perception confines soul awareness to the illusional sense of independent selfhood. After they have been wisely used to purify the mind and to accomplish samadhi without the support of an object of meditative contemplation, their renunciation allows complete enlightenment to be actualized.

52. Upon awakening to Self-knowledge there should be no pride or egotism in regard to spiritual status or attachment to it, as this can cause a return to former, unclear states of awareness.

When the ego is purified, the enlightened soul knows that Self-realization is not an attainment; it is the restoration of soul awareness to its original, clear state.

53. By meditative contemplation on moments of time and of sequential changes that occur, knowledge [of time and causation] born of discernment arises.

54. By discerning moments and sequential changes that occur, the difference between similar events that is not ordinarily observed is discerned.

When attention is diffused or awareness is unclear, one may mistakenly presume that similar events which occur at different moments of time, and have similar but different causes, to be the same. What occurs at any moment is unique to that moment because it corresponds to its specific cause.

55. Absolute discriminative knowledge is simultaneous knowledge of the entirety of the universe and its aspects and manifestations.

When we are cosmic conscious, awareness of omnipresence and omniscience that includes comprehensive knowledge of the reality of God and the various aspects, expressions, and processes of the universe is simultaneous.

56. When the purity of individualized awareness is the same as the purity of the Self, absolute liberation of consciousness is realized.

Only a portion of an egocentric soul's awareness identifies with mental and physical characteristics which modify it; the essence of being is always clear and tranquil. When egoism is replaced by Self-knowledge and individualized awareness is clarified, soul freedom results.

FOUR

Enlightenment and Liberation

1. Exceptional abilities and powers of perception may result from circumstances related to physical birth, biochemistry, mantras, practices that contribute to psychological transformation, and samadhi.

Circumstances related to birth include the degree of the soul's awareness when born, karmic influences of the incarnating soul and the parents, the basic mind-body constitution of the parents, and environmental factors. The wise use of foods, herbs, and other substances can influence biochemical processes and contribute to physical health, mental acuity, and clarification of awareness (see Glossary: *Ayurveda* and *rasayana*.) Mantras can purify the mind and influence and awaken kundalini energies. Practices that nurture psychological health result in rational thinking and clarify soul awareness. Frequent practice of samadhi weakens and removes subconscious conditionings, purifies the ego, unveils knowledge, and allows unrestricted application of awakened knowledge.

2. Transformation and refinement of the senses, mind, and body occurs because of the natural flow of the soul's creative forces.
3. Actions are not transformed into creative energies; they are performed to remove obstacles which inhibit the flow of creative forces.

Constructive lifestyle routines attune us with Nature's rhythms and energies and make us receptive to them. Effective spiritual practice removes obstructions to the flow of soul forces which transform and refine the senses, mind, and physical body.

4. Individualized fields of awareness are produced by the Cosmic Field of Awareness.
5. Although individualized fields of awareness are many and their activities are diverse, one Cosmic Field of Awareness originates them.

As there is but one Consciousness which individualizes to express as souls, so there is but one Mind which provides the mind-substance which is particularized and used by matter-identified souls.

6. Of modifications of individualized awareness, those produced by samadhi are devoid of karma.

Awareness modified or conditioned because of the accumulation of mental impressions (memories) of experience, perceptions, thoughts, feelings, and desires can be affected by those modifying influences, causing more karmic impressions to accumulate. Mental modifications produced by repeated superconscious episodes do not cloud awareness or cause destructive behaviors; they purify the mind by weakening and removing restrictive subconscious conditionings.

7. The karma [subliminal causative influences] of one for whom fluctuations of awareness are restrained is neither dark nor light; for others it is of three kinds.

For the spiritual aspirant who has stopped the actions of

subliminal urges and tendencies, karma is no longer influential. It neither obscures awareness nor contributes to its clarity. The karma of others (who have not subdued the actions of subliminal urges and tendencies) is classified as (1) karma which is presently influential or expressive; (2) karma which is being accumulated because of unregulated thoughts, disturbed emotional states, egocentric desires, and harmful actions; (3) dormant karmic tendencies yet to be influential which can be neutralized and eliminated.

8. The impulses and causative forces of karma are manifested when circumstances are most suitable for their expression.

Until the innate forces of latent subconscious desires, tendencies, and inclinations have been neutralized, there is always the possibility that they will be activated when circumstances which afford them an opportunity for expression are encountered. The wise devotee who is not satisfied with the accomplishment of only partial soul freedom will live skillfully and become increasingly proficient in experiencing superconscious states which will, in time, result in complete purification of the mind.

9. Because of the similarity of conscious thoughts and memories, feelings are aroused simultaneously with memories even though they may be separated by intervals in space and time.

When reminded of an event that occurred in the recent or distant past, it is not uncommon to also experience the feelings that accompanied the observation or the personal experience of that event. Seeing or hearing about an event can bring forth a surge of memories and feelings which have no direct relationship to what is perceived. Such feelings may be pleasurable; cause discomfort or mental confusion; or have no effect. Devotees who are committed to spiritual growth should learn to observe memories without emotional reaction to them.

10. Because of the life-urge to express which is innate to consciousness, there is no precise beginning to the flow of causes and their consequences.
11. Karmic patterns are maintained by their causes, the mind, and the support of objects of perception. In their absence, karmic patterns cease to exist.
12. Subliminal impressions of past events exist along with the potentiality of future events because of the exchange and transformation of cosmic forces.
13. Karma, whether dormant or presently expressive, is composed of the cosmic forces of Nature.
14. Because of the unified interactions of Nature's attributes, there is a unity of manifestations of Nature, events, and circumstances.

Combined attributes of Nature produce subconscious conditionings along with their driving forces stored in the mind, the repository of accumulated memories which comprise the karmic condition. The soul, being nonmaterial, does not accumulate karma. Karma can only be influential when awareness is identified with the mind and its conditioned characteristics. The ongoing manifestations and unique expressions of events and circumstances occurring in the universe are due to the coordinated interactions of Nature's three constituent attributes (*gunas*) which regulate cosmic forces.

15. How an object [a thought, idea, feeling, thing, or circumstance] is perceived is determined by the [powers

of] perception of the observer.

16. The existence of an object is not dependent upon the perception of one observer.

17. Objects are perceived according to how they affect or do not affect the awareness of the perceiver.

18. Because of the changeless nature of the Self, all modifications in its field of awareness are always known by it.

19. Because the mind is observed by the seer, it is not self-luminous.

The *seer*—the soul as the perceiver—being distinct from the mind, is alone self-luminous.

20. Simultaneous identification with the Absolute and relative phenomena is not possible.

The key word in this sutra is *identification*. While full awareness of relative phenomena and of the Absolute is possible when one is cosmic conscious, identification results in fixation and confinement of attention.

21. If the contents of all minds and individualized fields of awareness were simultaneously knowable to all other individualized fields of awareness, confusion of memories would result.

22. The one Consciousness is omnipresent, omniscient, omnipotent, and eternal. When reflections [souls] of Consciousness become involved with the material organ of intelligence, they identify with it.

When souls, units of the one Consciousness, fail to determine the distinction between themselves and the manifesta-

tions of cosmic forces they observe, their awareness is inclined
to identify with that which they observe. This primary intellectual error results in undiscerning involvement with mind and
matter.

23. Individualized awareness is influenced by both the
    observer and by that which is observed.

What we observe is impressed in the mind as a memory.
Our response (the thoughts and feelings that arise) to what we
observe also impresses the mind with memories and may even
cause a shift of mental attitude and state of awareness.

24. The mind, with its varied and numberless driving
    forces, exists to serve the Self.
25. One who discerns the difference between the body,
    senses, mind, and the Self, is liberated.

A selection from the Bhagavad Gita (3.42,43) describes the
soul's relationship to the mind. "The senses, some say, are
superior. [In truth] superior to the senses is the mind; superior
to the mind is the intellect; superior to the intellect is the Self.
Thus knowing this, sustaining Self-awareness by Self-knowledge, eliminate the obstacle of insistent desire [that is often so
difficult to overcome]."

26. Having overcome attachments to the body, senses, and
    mind, awareness becomes serene and flows in the
    direction of absolute freedom.
27. Even when attention is inclined in the direction of
    absolute freedom, interruptions of meditative contem-
    plation may occur during intervals when awareness
    is invaded by thoughts because of the influential force

of habits, subliminal tendencies, and memories.

28. One must dismiss and renounce these beliefs. Illusions, and fantasies are obstacles to enlightenment. Aspiration for liberation supports alert meditative contemplation and improves receptivity to samadhi.

29. When even the craving for liberation is renounced, innate knowledge unfolds.

Craving (needy desire) for liberation causes emotional distress, disturbs concentration, perpetuates the false notion of being separate from God, and inhibits spontaneous spiritual awakening. Aspiration for liberation supports alert meditative contemplation and improves receptivity to samadhi.

30. With the dawning of the knowledge that accompanies Self- and God-realization, all obstructions and restrictions cease to be influential.

31. With the dissolution of obstructions and restrictions, the Self reclaims omnipresence.

32. With the dawning of that knowledge, the cosmic forces, having served their purposes, cease to be influential.

Cosmic forces acting in the mind are influential in enabling us to acquire knowledge, experience, and spiritual growth. When we are enlightened, the support of cosmic forces for these purposes is no longer required.

33. [When] no longer perceiving changes from moment to moment, the Self is established in absolute knowledge beyond time and change.

34. When the cosmic forces, having no further purposes to serve, return to their primary state, the freedom of absolute Self-realization is actualized.

35. Fully enlightened, the soul is completely liberated.

The purpose of the actions of the cosmic forces in one's field of awareness is to support the actions of the mind. When the mind is calmed and subliminal influences cease, cosmic forces which were formerly supportive of the mind's actions return to their primary, dormant state.

36. Liberation is that state in which realization of pure consciousness is permanent.
37. Liberation is absolute when one Consciousness is perceived to exist and the universe and its processes are perceived as self-referring actions of the aspects of one Consciousness.
38. Supreme Consciousness with attributes [God] has the characteristics of consciousness, existence, and bliss. Absolute Supreme Consciousness is devoid of characteristics.

Here ends this exposition on yoga [samadhi].

Part Three

Introduction to
the Bhagavad Gita

The Culmination of Right Practice

For the accomplished devotee who is established in the yoga [samadhi] of realization of oneness, there is no further need to engage in strenuous procedures to accomplish psychological transformation, nor to perform rituals to support concentration or endeavor to invite the influences of beneficent forces. Therefore, diligently practice yoga [samadhi]. Of devotees who practice, that one who has dissolved the illusional sense of individuality into pure consciousness, and is surrendered in it, is firmly established in the highest realization.

– Bhagavad Gita 6:46,47

AUTHOR'S NOTE: Italics are used only when word definitions are provided or for special emphasis. Most of the text is from the Introduction of my book *The Eternal Way*, a spiritual interpretation of the Bhagavad Gita with commentary in the light of Kriya Yoga. Published by CSA Press.

The Inner Meaning of the Bhagavad Gita

The Bhagavad Gita, one of the great literary classics of the ages, has spiritually nurtured and inspired millions of its readers for over two thousand years. The common translation of the title is descriptive of a holy or divine song: Sanskrit *bhaj*, reverence or love, to share wealth and glory; and *gita*, from the verb-root *gai*, to sing. The prefix *srimad* (or *shrimat*), from the verb-root *sri*, to flame, to spread or pour out light, is usually used in the title.

The two central characters in the story are Arjuna and Krishna. *Arjuna* represents the seeker of knowledge and experience of God. *Krishna*, Arjuna's cousin, friend, teacher, and the personification of divine power and grace in human form, represents the indwelling Spirit of God. In eighteen chapters, a broad range of philosophical views are explored and practical instruction about how to live skillfully and fulfill personal destiny is methodically expounded. The inner message of the Gita explains how to awaken to Self-knowledge and God-realization.

Although many devotees presume the text to affirm God to actually be a cosmic person whose name is Krishna, a more insightful analysis reveals that, what is pointed to, is a supreme or transcendent Reality which, because formless and nameless, is beyond all categories, therefore, indescribable although knowable or realizable.

In the first ten chapters, *Jnana Yoga*, the way of knowledge; *Karma Yoga*, the way of selfless work or action; and *Bhakti Yoga*, the way of surrendered devotion to God, are described along with mind-freeing philosophical ideas. In the eleventh chapter, Arjuna, by Krishna's grace, is enabled to perceive the reality of the one Consciousness expressive as all things. The story does not end there; a cosmic conscious episode is but the beginning of a new and higher stage of life during which knowledge has to be applied and integrated into the fabric of existence. The concluding seven chapters are devoted to explaining how to apply in daily life what has been learned.

When read superficially, the text tells of a great war that occurred between opposing factions, who were cousins, on a battlefield north of the present-day city of New Delhi, India. When interpreted as an allegory—a story in which characters, objects, and events symbolically illustrate ideas or moral and spiritual principles—the esoteric meaning portrays a drama far more significant than any transitory historical event. The insightful reader is provided with the following helpful information: (1) the progress of the soul's awakening from self-conscious involvements with physical and psychological circumstances to realization of its true nature as pure consciousness; (2) the challenges commonly confronted during the process; (3) the liberating knowledge which removes awareness from all that is suppressive and restrictive.

The truths explained have great value to every person who sincerely aspires to clear understanding of life's processes and of ways to facilitate rapid, authentic spiritual growth that culminates in illumination of consciousness and soul liberation. Mind-clouded, sense-bound existence characteristic of ordinary human experience is often painful and sometimes seems to be devoid of meaningful purpose. What is needed, is for the mind to be illumined by the soul's innate light and for the senses to be subject to the soul's will or capacity to freely choose. Self-consciousness is then transcended and life flows smoothly under the direction of soul-originated impulses referred to as grace. The actions of grace are the effective influences of the inclination of the Spirit of God indwelling Nature to fulfill the purposes of life.

As soul-mind-body beings relating to the physical realm, we are instinctively and intuitively directed to fulfill basic desires and to satisfy needs essential to our survival, security, well-being, and continued growth. To this end, we innately want to live in harmony with Nature's processes, have life-enhancing desires easily fulfilled, experience spontaneous satisfaction of needs, and know of and unfold our spiritual potential. When soul awareness is not yet pronounced, we may be inclined to direct most of our attention to satisfying our physical and emotional needs and to ignore or neglect our spiritual growth. While this behavior may result in marginal human happiness, it will not satisfy the deep-seated desire of the heart (real essence of being) to awaken to that Self-knowledge which allows God-experience and transcendent realizations.

In Sanskrit literature, the first chapter serves as the introduction to the main body of the text. To have access to the core message, we have to carefully examine this chapter to acquire an understanding of the author's purpose for writing the Bhagavad Gita and learn the esoteric meanings of the names of the main characters of the story. In the lengthy Mahabharata epic, of which the Gita is but a small part, tradition and folklore are interwoven with symbolism in narrating the history of Bharata, an ancient King, and his descendents. The main characters of the drama are introduced in the following unusual ways:

In ancient India, at Hastinapur, there lived a king of the solar dynasty whose name was Santanu. The first of his two queens was named Ganga. When she deserted him under unusual circumstances, he wed Satyavati.

While walking beside the Ganges River, King Santanu met Ganga and asked her to be his wife. He did not then know that she was actually a manifestation of the river in human form. Ganga agreed to his proposal only after the King promised not to interfere with anything she might do after they married. If he ever questioned her actions, she declared, she would forsake him immediately.

When their first son was born, Ganga carried the infant from the palace and threw it into the river. The King, although much disturbed by her behavior, because of his prior promise not to interfere did not attempt to prevent it.

Six more sons were born, and each of them was given to the Ganges by the Queen. When the eighth son was born, the King implored her not to do with that infant as she had done with the first seven. True to her word, Ganga left her husband and her eighth son. Rushing to the Ganges River, she threw herself into it and merged in the waters.

King Santanu lavished affection upon his remaining son, Devavrata, providing for his education and training in all arts and skills befitting a prince and heir.

One day, the King went hunting in the forest. Resting under the shade of a tree by a river, he saw lotus petals floating on the waters. Following the stream of petals to their source, he saw a charming damsel, Satyavati, putting them into the river as a ritual offering.

Remaining out of the young woman's sight, the King followed her when she returned home, where she lived with her father, Dasa Raja, known as the fisher-king because his main activity was fishing. Santanu talked with Dasa Raja, requesting consent for Satyavati to be his wife.

Dasa Raja agreed, insisting, however, that his daughter must be the principal wife and that her son must be the successor to the throne.

King Santanu refused the terms of marriage and returned to his palace. As time passed, everyone around him became aware of his unhappiness. Prince Devavrata decided to do something about the situation. Without telling anyone of his plan, he went alone to Dasa Raja and asked him to consent to the marriage of Satyavati to his father. To reassure Dasa Raja about his daughter's future and that of any future sons, Prince Devavrata promised that he would not himself claim the throne, and that he would never marry or have any children. Because of these two awesome vows, Prince Devavrata thereafter became known as Bhishma (the formidable).

King Santanu and Satyavati were married. Two sons were born of their union: Chitrangada, who died at an early age, and Vichitravirya, who was peculiar and weak. After Santanu's demise, Vichitravirya became King, but because he was weak, the kingdom was really ruled by Bhishma.

When Vichitravirya grew to adulthood, Bhishma decided that he should have a queen. With this plan in mind, he went to the court of the King of Kashi, where a gathering of royal families assembled for the purpose of having their daughters choose husbands from among the princes who were invited to be there. The King of Kashi had three marriageable daughters. In keeping with the tradition of that time and culture—of sometimes kidnapping women for the purpose of marriage—Bhishma waited until the King's three daughters wandered away from the larger group, put them into his chariot, and rushed back toward Hastinapur.

The princesses' names were Amba, Ambika, and Ambalika. Amba prayed to be released because, in her heart, she had already promised herself to another. Bhishma let her go and continued on with the two remaining sisters.

King Vichitravirya, because of his weak constitution, died soon after marrying Ambika and Ambalika. His two widowed wives were then introduced to the sage Veda Vyasa, and by him each had a son. Ambika's son, Dhritarashtra, was born blind. Ambalika's son, Pandu, was of light complexion.

Bhishma continued to rule the kingdom. When the sons grew to adulthood, Pandu was put on the throne because Dhritarashtra, his older half brother who would have otherwise ruled, was blind.

Pandu had two wives, Kunti and Madri. Before her marriage, Kunti, testing the power of a mantra she had learned from a sage, inadvertently invoked the blessings of the sun and gave birth to a male child. Because it was considered to be illegitimate, the child was adopted by a carpenter and later became known as Karna, a hero of the Kaurava clan. After her marriage, Kunti invoked the gods who controlled *dharma* (righteous actions), *prana* (vital forces), and *Indra* (the god of fire, the power of transformation). From these unions were born Yudhisthira, Bhima, and Arjuna. Kunti then taught the mantra to Madri, who could only use it once. Madri invoked twin gods and begat twin sons, Nakul and Sahadeva. Because they were considered to be the progeny of Pandu, the five sons were known as the Pandavas.

When the five Pandava brothers grew to adulthood, they participated in a contest arranged by King Drupada for the purpose of having a husband chosen for his daughter, Draupadi. Participants in the contest had to lift a heavy bow, string it, and shoot an arrow through the eye of a fish that was hanging above a revolving wheel with a hole in the center. More, they had to aim at the target by looking into a reflection pool below. Arjuna, among all of the contestants, was successful. Returning to their home with Draupadi, the brothers asked Kunti, their mother, to come outside of the house to see what they had brought. She said, "Whatever you have brought, share among yourselves." Draupadi thus became the wife of the Pandavas.

The blind Dhritarashtra, half brother to King Pandu, fathered one hundred sons and one daughter, cousins to the five Pandava brothers. When King Pandu died, Duryodhana, the firstborn son of Dhritarashtra, sought the throne which he felt was rightfully his because his blind father had been denied it. When Yudhisthira, the eldest Pandava, was put on the throne instead, Duryodhana conspired to remove him from rulership of the kingdom. To do this, advised by a conspirator in the plot to use loaded dice, he challenged Yudhisthira to a dice game. It was agreed that whoever should lose would have to go into exile for twelve years, plus retire into seclusion for one year. Yudhisthira lost the game, and with his four brothers and their wife, Draupadi, departed for the agreed upon period of time. Duryodhana assumed rulership of the kingdom.

After thirteen years, the Pandava brothers returned to Hastinapur to reclaim their rights, but were refused them. Civil war was declared. All of the royal families of that region of India took sides and gathered their armies. Krishna, a king, and cousin of the Pandavas, asked the opposing factions to choose either him or his army. He would not participate in the battle, but would put his army at the disposal of whoever wanted it, while remaining with the other side.

What are we to think about this amazing story? We learn of a King who weds an embodiment of the Ganges River, who, for reasons of her own, throws her first seven sons into the water and merges into the river when she is not allowed to dispatch her eighth son as she did the first

Inner Meaning of the Progenitors of the Pandavas (*Chakras*)

Field of Absolute Pure Consciousness
King Santanu

Ganga, intelligence in Om produces eight manifestations (sons): Consciousness as the six inner regulating aspects, all-pervading Consciousness, and its individualized reflective aspect, *Bhishma*.

Satyavati, Om as primordial nature produces its aspects of time, space, and cosmic particles; *maya*, the energy-substance that manifests as the universe.

Chitrangada: manifesting primordial nature.
Vichitravirya: egoism; sense of independent existence.
Vyasa: power of discernment of relative circumstances.

Ambika: doubt, uncertainty   *Ambalika*: faculty of discrimination

Dhritarashtra: deluded mind   *Pandu*: pure intelligence

Duryodhana: base desire which is difficult to resist and its self-serving mental tendencies, the *Kurus*.

Kunti: dispassionate attraction.   *Madri*: sentimental attraction

Yudhisthira	Bhima	Arjuna	Nakula	Sahadeva
cervical chakra	dorsal chakra	lumbar chakra	sacral chakra	base chakra
ether element	air element	fire element	water element	earth element

Draupadi: *Kundalini shakti* that vitalizes the five *chakras*.

Note: The expressive aspects of Consciousness which manifest and enliven the universe also manifest and enliven the human body and all other biological forms. Pure Consciousness pervades the universe and is individualized as souls. The soul's unfolded Self-revealed knowledge returns its awareness to cosmic consciousness, realization of oneness, and liberation.

seven. We learn of plural marriages, children conceived by the power of mantra, manipulative behaviors, intrigue, deception, and finally, a decision to engage in battle. An interesting story! What can we learn from it? The key to understanding the drama is to discover what the names of the characters mean and what their actions and experiences reveal. To accomplish this, we have to review the story and examine the mythical genealogy and the unique behaviors of the participants in accord with the concepts of the philosophical system known as *Samkhya*—the precise numbering and classification of the categories of the emanations and manifestations of Consciousness:

Santanu, (pure Consciousness) interacted with *Ganga* (the conscious intelligence of Om). From this interaction, eight aspects of Consciousness were produced. The first seven always remain hidden or subjective; the eighth is objective.

The seven hidden aspects which regulate subjective cosmic processes are: two aspects, cosmic and individualized, at the level of causal or fine cosmic forces of creation; two aspects, cosmic and individualized, at the level of astral or subtle life forces; two aspects, cosmic and individualized, at the level of gross physical creation; and one all-pervading aspect. Although in some religious traditions these are referred to as gods, they are not independent beings; they represent the various intelligence-directed influences and powers of Consciousness.

In Vedic scriptures, the two aspects at the causal level are, together, referred to as *Vishnu*, that which preserves or maintains. The two aspects at the astral level are referred to as *Brahma*, that which expands and causes manifestation. The two aspects at the physical level are referred to as *Shiva*, that which causes change and transformation; also *Maheshvara*, the "great lord" or ruler. The seventh unseen aspect is the Spirit of

God pervading the cosmos without itself being confined to or limited by it.

The eighth aspect, which does not remain hidden, is cosmic individuality or *Bhishma* (the witness or perceiving aspect of Consciousness which participates in outer affairs but is not itself the determining factor. Because it is unmarried (aloof from creation), it does not produce anything. It and the Spirit of God are like two faces of Consciousness: the former looks outward into the realm of objective Nature, the latter remains hidden. The Sanskrit word for the all-pervading Spirit, the consciousness of God aspect, is *Kutastha Chaitanya*, "the one on the summit." It is sometimes referred to by Hindu devotees as Krishna Consciousness. Some devotees personalize it in order to feel themselves to be in close relationship to it.

Interacting with the unconscious side of Nature, *Satyavati* (the intelligent principles of primordial Nature—Om expressive as fine cosmic forces, space, and time—which embodies *sat* or truth), the enlivening aspect of Consciousness causes the primordial field of Nature, *maya*—that which is form-building and truth-veiling—to undergo changes which cause outward manifestation of itself. The first to manifest (the first child of Satyavati) is the aspect of the field of primordial Nature undergoing mutation from fine to gross expression which does not last long (*Chitrangada*). Satyavati's second son, *Vichitravirya* (the false or deluded sense of independent existence, ego consciousness) which, although peculiar (different) and weak, is necessary for the processes of creation to occur. Because it is contractive, it is relatively powerless. It conceals knowledge but is not possessed of knowledge.

The two wives of ego consciousness (*Vichitravirya*) are doubt (*Ambika*) and the power of discrimination (*Ambalika*). The other sister, *Amba*, chose not to marry because she was promised to another (involved with sensation through the lower chakras). In the story, Vichitravirya weakened and died soon after marrying his wives. It was then arranged for them to have children by the sage *Veda Vyasa* (wisdom-knowledge). From knowledge and doubt (*Ambika*) blind mind (*Dhritarashtra*) is born. From knowledge and the power of discrimination (*Ambalika*) pure intelligence (*Pandu*) is born.

In the Mahabharata story, it is said that Dhritarashtra and his wives had one hundred sons and a daughter. This means that blind or deluded mind, influenced by sentiment or feeling, produces numberless self-serving tendencies. The first of these was *Duryodhana* (passion, lower desire that is difficult to fight or resist, which causes many problems). Although Dhritarashtra and Pandu belonged to the Kuru clan, only Dhritarashtra became known as the chief representative of the clan because, with Bhishma's help, he ruled the kingdom.

Pandu (pure intelligence) with his two wives: *Kunti* (kundalini's power of attraction, dispassionate compassion, and discernment which banishes error) and *Madri* (intellect influenced by sentiment) secluded himself in the forest and was, therefore, away from the kingdom (of the mind). Yogis teach the front part of the body to be the realm of mental and physical impulses and tendencies. The back, the spinal pathway, rules spiritual inclinations. Dhritarashtra's children are referred to as *Kauravas* (representative of the self-serving, destructive or trouble-causing tendencies and habits rooted in the mind) which are considered to be enemies of the soul's aspiration to enlightened understanding. Pure intelligence, like Pandu in the story, remains aloof, while the mind, like Dhritarashtra, rules material affairs.

By the power of mantra, the two wives of Pandu produced five sons, referred to as the *Pandavas* (the products of pure intelligence). *Kunti* (kundalini's power of attraction, dispassionate compassion, and discernment which banishes error) produced three sons: Yudhisthira, Bhima, and Arjuna. They symbolize the true essences (*tattvas*) of the subtle elements of the three higher chakras in the spinal pathway.

Yudhisthira (righteousness, dharma, steadfast and firm) represents the ether element essence of the throat chakra at the cervical section of the spine: *Vishudda*, the pure. The sound frequency is of the ocean's roar, the mingling of all of the sounds of prana frequencies of the chakras. The color is misty grey with sparkling points of light. The taste is sour. The seed (*bija*) mantra, is *Ham* (pronounced "hum").

Bhima (dauntlessness, pranayama, control of vital forces, endless strength, formidable) represents the air element essence of the heart center at the dorsal section of the spine: *Anahata*, unstruck sound—like the peal of a gong. The color is blue. The taste is salty. The seed mantra is *Yam* ("yum").

Arjuna (purity of mind and heart, the aspiration to excellence, fiery self-control) represents the fire element essence of the lumbar chakra, midway between the higher and lower chakras: *Manipura*, the city of gems. The color is red. The sound frequency is as of a harp. The taste is pungent. The seed mantra is *Ram* ("rum").

Pandu's second wife, *Madri* (spiritual intellect influenced by sentiment), gave birth to twins, which symbolize the element influences of the two lower chakras:

Nakula (the stillness of the mind, the power to adhere) represents the water element essence of the chakra at the sacral region of the spine: *Swadisthan*, the abode of the Self. The color is of a white crescent moon. The sound frequency is of a flute. The taste is astringent. The seed mantra is *Vam* ("vum").

Sahadev (the power of resistance) represents the earth element essence of the chakra at the bottom of the spine: *Muladhara*, foundation. The color is yellow. The sound frequency is like the buzzing of disturbed bees. The taste is bitter. The seed mantra is *Lam* ("lum").

Draupadi, the common wife of the five Pandava brothers, represents *kundalini shakti*: the flowing, harmonizing, enlivening actions of the creative power of the soul expressive in the body. The five sons of Draupadi are the sound and light frequencies perceived in the chakras when they are energized by the actions of kundalini shakti.

The eldest Pandava brother, *Yudhisthira* (righteousness, tranquility) the fifth chakra state of consciousness, gambled with his eldest cousin, *Duryodhana* (egotism, lower desire, jealousy, pride), lost the match, and was banished. When righteousness plays with unrighteousness, when soul awareness gambles with conditioned mental tendencies and sense attractions, errors in judgment can occur, causing clouding of awareness. To reclaim the former status, one must withdraw for a duration to become grounded in the virtues, engage in spiritual practices, and again confront that which restricts the soul's freedom of expression and the fulfillment of its destiny; hence, the symbolism of the Pandavas having to be exiled, going into seclusion, and returning to engage in battle.

When Krishna (enlightened consciousness) offered his services to one of the opposing factions and his army to the other, the *Kauravas* (the self-serving mental tendencies) chose the army. The Pandavas chose Krishna, who agreed to drive Arjuna's chariot. The outcome of the forthcoming contest was then already decided, for where there is Krishna (enlightened consciousness), victory is certain.

Translating and commenting on the Bhagavad Gita requires alert attention to details regarding the intent of the original author[s]. It is believed by some scholars that, through the years, minor changes were made in the text and perhaps some additional material included. Also, for many centuries before the invention of the printing press, the entirety of the Mahabharata, which includes the eighteen chapters of the Gita, was communicated by storytellers who had memorized it. The elaborate, colorful, and often dramatic narration made it easy to remember and popular with people in all walks of life. Even without knowledge of its inner meaning, listeners (and, later, readers) could derive benefit at whatever level the message was comprehended. At an exoteric level, there is much of value to be learned in regard to meaningful human existence, the well-being of society, and the importance and usefulness of sustained spiritual aspiration. The esoteric message has value to those who are perceptive enough to understand and benefit from it. Because the concepts set forth in the story were already well-known when it was composed, the information is considered to be traditional, or remembered, knowledge rather than a new revelation. It is, however, accepted as an authentic Scripture of Yoga.

We must remember that the story begins as a great war between rival factions is about to start. The incidents described and the dialogue provided for the symbolic characters, portray the drama of individual psychological transformation and spiritual growth. The words attributed to Arjuna and Krishna, and of the few other characters who are given lines to speak, were written for the purpose of describing timeless truths.

Dhritarashtra represents unenlightened mind, the father of the physical aspects of Nature and ruler of the kingdom of the senses. Knowledge of transformative processes cannot be apprehended by a mind governed by partial understanding devoid of discernment. In the story, Dhritarashtra or deluded mind is blind and at a place distant from where the armies have gathered; he relies on his counselor, Sanjaya, to report on what is transpiring. Sanjaya, with powers of clairvoyance which enable him to see with inner vision, represents every person's faculty of impartial intuitive perception that, when called upon during interludes of introspection, provides insight. The story begins with Dhritarashtra's question:

> Assembled on dharmakshetra-kurukshetra, desirous to fight, what did my sons and the sons of Pandu do, Sanjaya?

Dharma is righteousness, virtue, morality: that which upholds or supports evolution's inclination toward transformation, growth, and expression. The impulses of Consciousness which enhance life are dharmic. *Kshetra* is the field (place) where actions occur. The word *kuru* is used to refer to the characteristics and tendencies of the deluded mind. This first verse sets the stage for the drama which is to take place in the field where righteousness confronts unrighteousness. Where is this field? Since the story describes the soul's return of awareness to wholeness, the place where righteousness must overcome unrighteousness is the devotee's individualized awareness.

Arjuna's questions and comments testify to the soul's aspiration to awaken to Self-knowledge and realization of God, and of its conflicts, struggles, and endeavors to learn what is true and how to actualize it. In the story, Arjuna is portrayed as a warrior who must fulfill his duty in a responsible manner. He represents the soul at a critical stage of spiritual growth, still somewhat grounded in physical and mental awareness and its concerns (third chakra characteristics), yet beginning to awaken to higher understanding. The progression of unfoldment is from confusion to the fourth chakra, devotee stage devoid of ego-fixation; the fifth chakra stage of apprehension of truth (the facts of life); the sixth chakra stage of revelation; and final unfoldment of innate knowledge that culminates in permanent illumination of consciousness.

Krishna represents the accessible, grace-imparting reality of God that, while ever omnipresent, omniscient, and omnipotent, is also the indwelling reality of every soul and creature. Krishna's words are not to be thought of as the actual words of a historical personage; they represent Self-revealed knowledge that unfolds from the innermost level of being when one is prepared to recognize and comprehend it.

When reading the Gita, instead of thinking of the events described in the story as having occurred at another place and time, or the characters as real people, remember that what is described is every person's quest for understanding and personal endeavor to experience the unfoldment of innate potential. When reading the words attributed to Arjuna, you may recognize some of your own characteristics and attitudes. When reading statements attributed to Krishna, you are being reminded of the mind-cleansing, soul-liberating knowledge you already have within you.

Part Four

The Lineage of Teachers
of This Kriya Yoga Tradition

Babaji
Lahiri Mahasaya
Sri Yukteswar
Paramahansa Yogananda

The author, at Center for Spiritual Awareness headquarters. Background (*left*) portraits of Babaji and Lahiri Mahasaya; (*right*) Sri Yukteswar and Paramahansa Yogananda.

The Lineage of Teachers
of This Kriya Yoga Tradition

This Kriya Yoga tradition is transmitted by a lineage of gurus who are spiritually attuned to a master of yoga known as Babaji. Secluded in a remote region of the Himalayan Mountains in northern India, Babaji's twofold mission is to support the processes of planetary evolution in our current era and to assist people in all walks of life to more quickly awaken to conscious knowledge of their innate divine nature.

Sri Yukteswar met Babaji on three occasions, the first time in 1894. Babaji told Sri Yukteswar that he would send him a disciple who would take the message of yoga to the West. That disciple was Paramahansa Yogananda. In 1920, as my guru prepared to travel to America, he prayed for guidance. Babaji came to his home in Calcutta, assured him that his mission would be successful, and said, "Kriya Yoga will spread to all lands. It will aid in the harmonizing of the nations through humanity's personal, transcendental perception of the Infinite."

In recent years, a few individuals have published books and articles in which they claimed to have met Babaji in the Himalayas or that he appeared to them in a vision and instructed them to teach. So far as I know, none of them has had actual contact with him.

Lahiri Mahasaya

Shyamacharan Lahiri was born on September 30, 1828. The title, *Mahasaya* (one who is cosmic conscious), was used by his disciples. Married, the father of five children, in his adult years he years lived in the ancient city of Banaras (now Varanasi), and was employed as a clerk by a department of the British government which supplied materials for road building projects.

In 1861 Lahiri traveled to Ranikhet in the foothills of the Himalayas, where he met Babaji and was initiated. During the next two weeks, he acquired proficiency in meditation practice and experienced several episodes of transcendent samadhi states. At Lahiri's request, Babaji agreed that the restrictions regarding yogic initiation could be somewhat modified to allow all sincere devotees of God to learn the principles and practices of Kriya Yoga. In the years that followed, Lahiri initiated more than five thousand disciples.

Twenty-two books of commentaries on various scriptures were written and published by this quiet yogi. Although he discouraged publicity regarding his mission, several spiritually qualified disciples of good character were authorized to initiate others and a few renunciate disciples established modest ashrams.

On the 26th of September 1895, in the presence of a few disciples, after expounding for several hours on the Bhagavad Gita, Lahiri Mahasaya sat upright and said, "I am going home." Absorbed in samadhi, he consciously left his body. Cremation rites were performed at Manikarnika Ghat by the Ganges River.

Swami Sri Yukteswar

Priya Nath Karar was born on May 10, 1855. In his early adult years, he married, attended college classes for a while, managed rental properties inherited from his father, and worked for a brief time as an accountant. His wife died at an early age after their only child, a daughter, was born. His monastic name, Yukteswar ("united with Ishwara," the ruling aspect of God in relationship to Nature) was assumed when he entered the swami order. He established two ashrams: in Serampore, near Calcutta, and Puri on the Bay of Bengal.

A master of yoga, Sri Yukteswar was also an accomplished vedic astrologer and possessed extensive knowledge of Ayurveda. He wrote two books: *The Holy Science* and a commentary on the first six chapters of the Bhagavad Gita. Because of his guru's highly developed powers of intelligence and intuitive insight, Paramahansa Yogananda often reverently referred to him as a *Jnanavatar*, an "incarnation of wisdom."

Sri Yukteswar seldom openly displayed his yogic powers, preferring instead to give helpful advice to others while assisting them in subtle ways to improve their lives. Compassionate and reserved, his devotional nature was not always apparent. His manner of speaking was direct, with emphasis on the necessity of moral, intellectual, and spiritual development and practical application of knowledge and functional skills.

Sri Yukteswar's mahasamadhi was on March 9, 1935. His body was buried in the garden of his Puri ashram. Several years later, a modest shrine was constructed on the site by his disciples.

Paramahansa Yogananda

Mukunda Lal Ghosh was born at Gorakhpur, India, on January 5, 1893. In his first year, his parents, both devoted disciples of Lahiri Mahasaya, took him to their guru to be spiritually baptized. At that time, Lahiri said, "Your son will be a great spiritual engine and carry many souls to God."

Before entering college, Mukunda met Sri Yukteswar and was initiated into Kriya Yoga practices. A few years later, when initiated into the renunciate order of swamis by Sri Yukteswar, he chose Yogananda (*yoga*, union; *ananda*, bliss) as his monastic name. *Paramahansa* is a title used for yogis who are highly God-realized.

Traveling to America in 1920, using the name Swami Yogananda, he lectured and presented classes in Boston, Massachusetts. He then toured several major cities, teaching the philosophy and practices of yoga to thousands of men and women. In 1925, during a highly successful lecture series in Los Angeles, he founded the international headquarters of the Self-Realization Fellowship, on Mount Washington, near the Highland Park district of Los Angeles. In the third and fourth decades of the 20th century, my guru lectured and conducted classes in southern California, trained disciples, and wrote many of his books.

Paramahansaji retired from public activities early in 1951. At his secluded retreat house in Twenty Nine Palms, California, he met with a few disciples and wrote his extensive commentary on the Bhagavad Gita. I visited him there several times, in his living room during the evening hours or while walking with him on the property.

During my last visit with Paramahansaji, he advised

me, "Don't allow your mind to be influenced by the words
or behaviors of others. Don't dwell on the past, or look to
the left or to the right. Look straight ahead. You must go
all the way in this incarnation—and you can!" He then
told me of his thoughts and feelings in regard to Sri
Yukteswar's mahasamadhi many years before, and gently hinted at his own soon passing.

On March 7, 1952, while at the Self-Realization Fellowship Center in Phoenix, Arizona, where I served as
the assistant minister, a brother disciple telephoned late
in the evening. "Master left his body," he said. I conducted
a memorial service for our members in Phoenix before traveling to California.

Several months prior to his passing, Paramahansaji
confided to a few disciples that his mission had been successfully accomplished: the organization he founded was
established on a firm basis and he had prepared successors to represent him. On March 7, he attended a dinner,
arranged in honor of India's Ambassador to the United
States, Binay Ranjan Sen. Concluding a short talk with a
recitation of one of his poems, my guru lifted his eyes and
left his body. Years before, he had said, "When I go, I want
to go while speaking of God and the masters." His body
was placed in a crypt at Forest Lawn Memorial-Park in
Los Angeles.

He told disciples that his teachings and spiritual influence would continue to benefit truth seekers for centuries. To those who asked about their future relationship
with him, he said, "If you think me near, I will be near."

Only a few people know that the wholeness
of God extends fully to this Earth realm.
Mahavatar Babaji

At the spiritual eye, God's light shines.
The spiritual eye is the door that leads the soul's
awareness into the realm of the divine glory of God.
God can be known when one enters the sanctuary
of pure, illumined consciousness.
Lahiri Mahasaya

God is without beginning or end, complete and
eternal, the one indivisible reality. If you desire
something with concentrated intention, even if it does
not yet exist, the universe will manifest it for you.
Sri Yukteswar

If you want God's guidance in your life, don't waste
your time in idle talk. Silence is the altar of Spirit.
Let your devotion to God be like a wood fire that
burns steady for a long time; not like a straw fire
that produces a bright flame and quickly dies out.
In the highest state of Self-realization you can
maintain awareness of God while working, speaking,
and moving about in this world. When this state is
perfected, there is no possibility of falling from it.
Paramahansa Yogananda

Glossary

Glossary

Absolute The transcendent field of pure Consciousness.

actualize To make real or bring into manifestation. Abilities are actualized when they are expressed or demonstrated. Goals are actualized when they are accomplished. Purposes are actualized when they are fulfilled.

advaita Nonduality. When the faculty of intellectual determination is purified and intuition is unveiled, the universe is apprehended as a continuous, undivided or whole manifestation of interacting cosmic forces originated and emanated by one unbounded field of Consciousness.

agni Fire. One of five primary element influences in Nature characterized by its transformative influence, including psychological and biochemical transformations. The *tejas* aspect of agni energizes the mind, manifests the radiance of health in the body, and influences eyesight. Agni is also evident as the divine force and illumined will that can manifest the soul's potential for growth and expression.

agnosticism The theory that, while not denying the existence of God, asserts that God cannot be known. An agnostic adheres to the opinion that only perceived phenomena are objects of exact knowledge. See *atheism* and *deism*.

ahamkara The illusional sense of "I-ness," self-identity. When the soul does not discriminate between itself as pure consciousness and its illusional sense of selfhood, a mistaken presumption of independent existence results.

ashram A quiet, secluded abode for study and spiritual practice. An ashram provides a supportive environment in which spiritual aspirants can live close to Nature without distractions. Only elevating influences should prevail, to nurture soul qualities and encourage their unfoldment.

astral realm The realm of life forces. Souls come from this realm into physical incarnation and return to it between Earth sojourns. Spiritually advanced souls may pass through it to continue their awakening in finer causal realms, or transcend involvement with all aspects of primordial Nature. See *causal realm*.

atheism Disbelief in or denial of the existence of God. See *agnosticism* and *deism*.

atman Or *atma*. The true or real, permanent essence of every person and creature. The individualized field of awareness, which, when matter- and mind-identified, is referred to as a soul. The word *Atman* with an upper case *A* is used to refer to the Supreme Being: *Paramatman* (*para*, beyond), the field of unmodified pure Consciousness.

avatar The emergence and manifestation of divine qualities and powers in human form. A full incarnation of God expressing for the purpose of infusing planetary consciousness with divine influences. Avatars are said to occasionally play dramatic roles, or their spiritual state may be unrecognized by those with whom they associate. Their redemptive work is in accord with the innate inclinations of impulses expressing as evolutionary trends and actions. The "universal avatar" concept is that, because the reality of God is individualized as every soul, divine capacities are unveiled when individual and collective consciousness is illumined.

avidya Not-knowledge, in contrast to *vidya*: knowledge of God's reality and its aspects and categories of manifestation.

Ayurveda *Ayus*, life; *veda*, knowledge. A natural way to nurture total well-being that evolved in India thousands of years ago. According to tradition, it was taught to man by the gods. Ayurvedic diagnostic procedures include examination of the patient's pulse, temperature, skin condition, eyes, psychological characteristics, behavior, and other factors. Treatment includes recommendations of foods and herbs for specific purposes, attitude adjustment, behavior modification, detoxification regimens, meditation practice, and other procedures applied to restore balance to the patient's mind-body constitution.

Lifestyle regimens are prescribed to balance the three *doshas*, the subtle governing principles (space-air, *vata*; fire, *pitta*; water-earth, *kapha*) which determine physiological functions and influence psychological states. Foods are recommended according to how their tastes (sweet, sour, salty, pungent, bitter, and astringent) influence the governing principles. Food transformation is said to progress through seven stages: plasma, blood, muscle, fat, bone, reproductive essences, and a refined vital essence (*ojas*).

In the *Charaka Samhita*, a primary Ayurvedic text, over five hundred herbs are listed with descriptions of their medicinal uses. From India, knowledge of Ayurveda flowed to Tibet, China, and Mediterranean countries, and finally to the West. During the years of British rule, although state patronage resulted in the decline of Ayurvedic practice in the urban centers of India, it continued to be the treatment of choice among rural populations. There are now several Ayurvedic colleges in India and in other countries, and scientific research is underway to investigate and endeavor to validate these wellness procedures.

Siddha Medicine, a similar wellness system, evolved in the southern region of India. Its many texts are believed to have been written by enlightened saints, among whom Agastya is especially revered. Practitioners of Siddha Medicine regimens may also prescribe the use of the ashes of gems and purified metals for healing and rejuvenation purposes. Thousands of years ago, yogis researched, discovered and used various means of ensuring healthy, long life for the purpose of allowing them to accomplish soul liberation. Some of their knowledge was made available for the welfare of people in secular society. See *ojas*.

Babaji *Baba*, father; *ji*, a suffix used at the end of a name to indicate respect. In Asia, many venerated male saints are referred to as Baba or Babaji. Mahavatar (*maha*, great; *avatar*) Babaji is the name used to refer to an enlightened saint who revived the ancient Kriya Yoga teachings and practices and made them more widely available in India during the nineteenth century. A woman saint may be addressed as Mataji (*mata*, mother; *ji*, who is reverenced).

Bhagavad Gita Holy or Divine Song. From *bhaj*, to revere or love; *gita*, song. A scripture treasured by millions of people in which Krishna is portrayed as a divine incarnation who teaches his disciple Arjuna "the eternal way of righteousness" and the ways of knowledge, selfless service, devotion, and meditation. Frequent reading of the Bhagavad Gita can purify the mind and awaken innate spiritual qualities. For an introduction to this text, see *Part Three*.

Bhagavan Lord, that which rules. Also, one who is endowed with the spiritual attributes of infinite spiritual power, righteousness, glory, splendor, knowledge, and renunciation.

bhakti Fervent, devoted love for God which can result in God-realization and acknowledgment and perception of the innate divinity of every person and creature. Love purifies the mind and unveils the soul's qualities.

bliss The unadulterated joy of awareness of pure being, rather than mental happiness or an emotional mood.

Brahma The expanding, projecting aspect of the Godhead which results in full manifestation of Nature. *Vishnu* is the name for the aspect of God which preserves and maintains the universe. *Shiva* is the name for God's transformative aspect which dissolves forms and circumstances to allow new expressions. *Shiva* is also considered to be Supreme Consciousness. *Shakti*, the cosmic creative energy of Supreme Consciousness, is referred to as its feminine expression that manifests and enlivens the worlds.

brahmacharya *Brahma*; divine; *charya*, going. Disciplined regulation of vital forces; mental, sensory, and emotional tendencies; and behaviors—for the purpose of conservation, wise use, and transmutation of energies, freeing them to be used for intentional living and dedicated spiritual practices. Transmuted energies increase reserves of *ojas*: refined energy that contributes to overall health and vitality.

Brahman The Supreme Reality, the Absolute.

Buddha A seer who lived in northern India about 500 BCE. Of royal birth, as a young man he became troubled when he learned of the sufferings of the average person in society. After marrying, and fathering a son, he left home to seek higher knowledge. Following a duration of ascetic yogic practice he adopted "the middle way" of reasoned moderation and awakened to illumination of consciousness. The word *buddha*, is used to refer to one who is enlightened. After his illumination he walked through the Ganges Valley for almost half a century, preaching and forming a society of renunciates. He taught love, nonhatred, dedication to truth, the elimination of wishful thinking, and nondependence upon externals. In Buddhism, spiritual enlightenment is viewed as that realization of the True Self which is common to all.

buddhi From the verb-root *budh*, to know. The faculty of discernment, the intellectual capacity. Because all souls are expressions of one Consciousness, all have a "buddha nature". When the true nature is directly experienced, *nirvana*, the "extinguishing" of the illusional sense of selfhood results.

capacity The capability to receive or contain. The power or ability to use skills and accomplish purposes. Right living and spiritual practices increase one's capacity to accomplish purposes and to more easily apprehend and experience the reality of God.

causal realm The realm of electric and magnetic properties preceding astral and physical manifestation. Souls reside here before returning to astral incarnation, or while awakening to transcendent levels. See *astral realm*.

chakra An astral vital center through which life forces flow. The first chakra (*muladhara*, "foundation") at the base of the spine represents the earth element. Its taste (which may be experienced in the meditator's mouth or throat when meditating on it or when its actions influence biochemical processes) is sweet; its color is yellow; its sound-vibration is like the noise of buzzing bees. The characteristic psychological states related to this chakra are restlessness, insecurity, and attachments.

The second chakra (*svadhisthan*, "abode of the self") at the sacral region of the spine represents the water element. Its taste is astringent; its color is white; its sound-vibration is perceived as being flutelike. The psychological state related to the second chakra is characterized by desire, sensuousness, and inclinations to discover one's self-identity.

The third chakra (*manipura*, "the city of gems") at the lumbar region of the spine represents the fire element. Its taste is bitter; its color is red; its sound-vibration is perceived as being similar to the sound of a harp. The psychological state related to this chakra is characterized by egocentric inclinations and strong powers of will.

The fourth chakra (*anahata*, "unstruck sound") at the dorsal region of the spine represents the air element. Its taste is sour; its color is blue; its sound-vibration is perceived to be like the flowing peal of a gong. The psychological state related to this chakra is characterized by aspiration to spiritual growth, which may be frustrated because powers of discernment are sometimes flawed.

The fifth chakra (*vishudda*, "pure") at the cervical region of the spine opposite the throat represents the ether element. Its taste is pungent; its color is grey or misty with sparkling points of light; its sound-vibration is perceived as thunder or the ocean's roar. The psychological state related to this chakra is characterized by inspiration to acquire knowledge.

The sixth chakra (*ajna*, "command" or "control") is the spiritual eye between the eyebrows which reflects the light of vital forces in the medulla oblongata at the base of the brain. It may be perceived as a ball of brilliant, white light, or as a dark blue field of light with a golden halo. A starlike light may be perceived in the blue field.

The seventh chakra (*sahasrara*, "thousand rayed") is in the higher brain, though not confined to it. Its radiance is white and brilliant "like a thousand suns." When one's awareness is identified with the six and seventh chakras, psychological states are transcended. When meditating with attenton focused at these chakras, the sound of Om may be heard prior to experiencing transcendent states.

chitta Pure Consciousness, the individualized Self identified with the mind, its contents, and transformations. The natural state of the Self is samadhi.

chitti Pure Consciousness.

Christ Latin *christus*; derived from Greek *kristos* (*khristos*, anointed, and *kriein*, to anoint). For secular purposes the word was used to refer to the religious rite of anointing with oil. In some Western philosophical systems, the aspect of God pervading the universe is referred to as Christ Consciousness because the manifest realms are considered to be "anointed" with God's Presence. Thus, one who has realized the all-pervading reality of God may be said to be Christ-conscious.

consciousness Ordinarily considered to be the state of being conscious or aware. The metaphysical meaning is that consciousness is the reality of God's being, souls, and all aspects and forms of Nature.

cosmic consciousness Awareness—which may be partial or complete—of Consciousness and its varied aspects as a continuum or wholeness. Cosmic consciousness usually unfolds gradually along with Self-revealed innate knowledge. It can be nurtured by renouncing egocentric attitudes and self-conscious behaviors, aspiration to spiritual growth, prayer, superconscious meditation, and reliance upon God. When meditative superconscious states continue during ordinary waking states, cosmic consciousness unfolds. Cosmic conscious states can also emerge suddenly.

Cosmic Mind The one Mind of which individualized minds are aspects or parts. Mind, whether Cosmic or individualized, includes: a field of awareness, self-sense (ego); the intellect or faculty of discernment; and the aspect which processes information—*manas*, that which thinks. Through its mind, the embodied soul is in relationship to Cosmic Mind. Our mental states, subliminal tendencies, thoughts, desires, and intentions interact with Cosmic Mind which is inclined to manifest corresponding conditions and circumstances.

deism Belief that God created the universe, but is removed from it, has no influence on phenomena, and provides no supernatural revelation. See *agnosticism* and *atheism*.

delusion An erroneous or invalid belief or opinion due to intellectual error; imperfect or incomplete discernment. The initial error of the intellect, from which all other delusions and their consequences result, is that of presuming the Self to be mind or matter. See *ego, illusion*, and *tapasya*.

deva That which shines, a god. In some philosophical systems the gods (*devas*) and goddesses (*devis*) are considered to be spiritually radiant souls dwelling in subtle or celestial realms. They are more accurately defined as the cosmic forces that regulate universal processes and can be invited to influence human affairs.

dharma That which upholds and supports the universe and empowers its evolutionary processes. To live righteously, appropriately, and correctly is to live in accord with its actions. To adhere to a known life-path in accord with the orderliness of the universe is to fulfill one's personal *dharma*.

disciple Word origin: Latin *discipulus*, pupil, student, learner; from *discere*, to learn. A disciple is committed to learning as an adherent of a philosophical system or spiritual tradition. See *guru*.

ego Mistaken self-identity because of intellectual error and the veiling or clouding of awareness that causes an illusional sense of being separate from God. Inaccurate self-perception is the basis of egoism. The soul, then presuming itself to be separated from its origins, identifies with fragmented states of awareness. *Egoism* is the condition of being egocentric. *Ego-*

tism is an extreme or exaggerated sense of self-importance often characterized by arrogance and self-centered willfulness. When the misperception of "I-ness" is corrected, the soul, while aware of being individualized, is not confined to or limited by that viewpoint. See *delusion* and *illusion*.

ether Space comprised of fine cosmic forces which are not yet matter but which have the potential to manifest as matter. The four other subtle element influences are air, fire, water, and earth, which interact to express as their corresponding material manifestations. The five subtle element influences are the true essences (*tattwas*) of the manifest universe. Physical manifestation of the elements occurs when half of one subtle element influence is mixed with one eighth part of each of the other four subtle element influences.

God The Supreme Being. The outer manifestation of Divine Consciousness with attributes and qualities, expressing in the direction of universal manifestation. The Oversoul.

guna A quality or attribute of Consciousness that regulates Nature's forces. The three gunas are the constituent aspects of the whole of Nature that determine its actions. *Sattva guna* contributes to purity and luminosity. *Rajas guna* contributes to movement and transformation. *Tamas guna* contributes to heaviness and inertia; its influence clouds the mind and prevails in the material realm. See *maya*.

guru Teacher. That which removes darkness or ignorance of the truth. The light and reality of God is the true guru that removes unknowingness from the mind and awareness of the disciple. An enlightened teacher is a *Satguru* (*sat*, the truth of being; *guru*, teacher-truth-revealer). See *disciple*.

heart The physical heart is the hollow muscular organ in the thoracic cavity that pumps blood into arteries to supply the circulatory system. The philosophical meaning is "the vital part of one's being, emotions, and sensibilities; the true Self or soul." When seer's advise, "Seek the truth in your heart," they mean that the reality of one's being is to be meditatively contemplated, discovered, and experienced.

heaven Originally a cosmological term used to refer to a region of the universe, which also came to function as a vehicle of religious idealism. In ancient Middle Eastern thought, heaven was imagined as a region of the observable cosmos which pointed beyond itself to a transcendent realm. In ancient Greek mythology, Zeus dwells on Mount Olympus. Writers of the books of The Old Testament referred to heaven as God's abode from which sovereign rule is exercised and to which the faithful righteous are finally welcomed. The New Testament reflects a modified version in which heaven is a creation of God in which God resides, as well as a condition of blessedness experienced by the spiritually prepared. Various sects have their concepts of heaven and its opposite place or condition. Illusion-free understanding allows one to directly experience the truth that degrees of Self-knowledge and God-realization determine personal circumstances.

humility The absence of egotism or arrogance.

illusion Misperception: failure or inability to accurately apprehend what is subjectively or objectively observed. Illusions which are believed to be true are delusions which distort awareness and contribute to mental and emotional conflict. When illusions are removed, soul awareness is restored to wholeness. See *ego*, *delusion*, and *tapasya*.

imagination Mental picturing or visualization of that which is not present to the senses. *Creative* imagination differs from daydreaming or fantasy only in degree. Disciplined imagining enables one to clearly define mental concepts and to envision possibilities of actualizing desired circumstances.

initiation Latin *initium*, beginning; from *inire*, to go in. A rite of passage which admits one into a body of knowledge and the company of adherents of that knowledge. When initiated into Kriya Yoga practices, the guru or the guru's representative imparts instruction in advanced meditation methods and recommended lifestyle regimens. The disciple, whose soul forces are quickened at the time of initiation, is encouraged to maintain a regular schedule of practice and to nurture mental and spiritual attunement with the gurus of the tradition.

Ishwara Or *Isvara*. The aspect of God which governs and regulates creation. Referred to as the lord or ruling influence.

japa Repetition of a mantra or any of the names of God for the purpose of cultivating devotion and improving meditative concentration. A *japmala* is a string of beads used to count the repetitions or to more completely involve the meditator's attention when engaged in prayerful contemplation. The rosary used by devout Catholics serves this purpose.

jivanmukta One who is soul- (*jiva*) liberated (*mukta*) while embodied. Although traces of karma (subliminal impressions) may remain, the soul is free because Self-realized. Future actions of the liberated soul are determined by it's innate intelligence, choices, and responsiveness to grace, rather than by karmic compulsion. A *paramukta* (*para*, beyond) is fully liberated, without delusions, illusions, or karmic compulsions. See *salvation*.

jnana Knowledge, especially knowledge of God.

jyotish The study and application of knowledge of astronomy and astrology. In the *Kaushitaki Brahmana*, an ancient treatise, it is indicated that in 3100 BCE Vedic scholars had knowledge of astronomy which they used to determine favorable times for religious ceremonies. Vedic astrologers calculate planetary positions in relationship to fixed signs.

In this system, certain gemstones are believed to radiate forces similar to those of the major planets, hence the reason for sometimes recommending their use to counteract or to strengthen planetary influences. Ruby is recommended for the influence of the Sun; pearl or moonstone for the Moon; red coral for Mars; emerald for Mercury; yellow sapphire for Jupiter; diamond for Venus; blue sapphire for Saturn; hessonite garnet and chrysoberyl cat's eye for the influences of the north and south nodes of the Moon. The use of gemstones for therapeutic or other helpful purposes should be prescribed by a spiritually enlightened astrologer.

kalpa An Age or duration of time. See *yuga*.

karma From the verb-root *kri*, to act; to do; to make [happen]. That which can cause effects. Subliminal influences and tendencies, habitual thoughts, mental states, states of consciousness, and actions determine personal experiences. The accumulation of mental and emotional memory impressions in the mind and physical body comprise the karmic condition. *Parabdha karma* is the residue of subliminal impressions which may be instrumental in causing future effects. If their potential effects are known to be harmless, they can be allowed to express, thus weakening and exhausting their motive force. They can be neutralized and dissolved by constructive living, surrendered prayer, meditation, repeated superconscious (samadhi) episodes, and the superior force of God-realization. See *samskara*.

kaya-kalpa A regimen for physical and mental rejuvenation and longevity described in Ayurvedic and Siddha Medicine literature. Procedures include routines for internal cleansing and for balancing the governing principles that determine the basic mind-body constitution, prolonged rest, a specific dietary regimen, and extended periods of meditation. To ensure seclusion, the subject usually remains in a quiet dwelling in a natural setting removed from social activities. Vitalizing substances and herbs may be used. Care is taken to provide circumstances which will allow Nature's healing forces and the soul's regenerative capacities to be influential. It is reported that by this process some saints have retained their physical bodies for hundreds of years. The most nourishing influences are provided by prolonged, meditative superconscious states. See *Ayurveda* and *rasayana*.

kriya Action, activity, process, procedure. Kriyas are actions performed to facilitate wellness, success, fulfillment, or restoration of soul awareness to wholeness; also, the spontaneous, transformative actions which may occur when kundalini energies (*shakti*) become expressive.

Kriya Yoga *Kriya*, action; *yoga*, to join or unite. Practices and processes that restore soul awareness to wholeness. In the teaching tradition of Babaji, Lahiri Mahasaya, Sri Yukteswar, Paramahansa Yogananda, and his successors, Kriya Yoga practices include wholesome lifestyle regimens and the use of specific meditation techniques that enable the practitioner to regulate flows of vital force, calm mental restlessness, purify the intellect, refine the nervous system and body, and effectively practice meditative contemplation. See *kriya* and *yoga*.

kundalini Dormant creative energy potential in Nature and in the body. When it awakens in Nature, life forms emerge and are enlivened. When it awakens in human beings, soul qualities unfold, psychological transformation occurs, intellectual capacities and intuitive powers are improved, exceptional abilities may be acquired, and superconscious and transcendent states may be spontaneously experienced.

Lahiri Mahasaya A disciple of Mahavatar Babaji and the guru of Sri Yukteswar. (September 30, 1828—September 26, 1895.) Living quietly, attending to family, work, and community duties, he offered instruction in Kriya Yoga practices to sincere truth seekers in all walks of life.

love The influence of Consciousness that unveils the mind's faculties of perception and releases the soul from bondage to mind and matter. The attracting and unveiling influence referred to as love is an expressive aspect of God. It is common to speak of love of country, love of mankind, love for others, and of love when referring to emotional affection and sentimental attractions. Pure love is healing, redemptive, elicits innate soul qualities, and invites surrender to and participation with the highest and best of all relationships.

mantra *Manas*, mind, that which thinks; *tra*, to protect. A meditation mantra is a meaningful, potent word or word-phrase that serves as an attractive focus of attention, displacing awareness from mental processes and allowing pure consciousness to be directly experienced.

master Latin *magister*, one who is proficient. A master of yoga (samadhi) has acquired control over sensory impulses, vital forces, mental states, and states of consciousness.

maya That which measures, defines, limits, and produces forms. The primary substance of Nature, the components of which are: vibrating creative force (*Om*), space, time, and cosmic forces which are not yet matter but which can manifest as matter when the actions of the three constituent attributes of Nature (gunas) are influential. Because of its form-producing inclination, maya is sometimes referred to as Divine Mother or Mother Nature. Another characteristic is that of veiling or obscuring the soul's faculties of perception. When a soul identifies with the field of Nature, its intuitive and intellectual capacities are blurred or obscured. Maya, although illusory, is not an illusion. It is the substance of everything in the field of objective Nature. See *guna*.

meditation An uninterrupted flow of attention to an object of concentration. Sustained meditation results in contemplation. In accord with the meditator's intention, contemplation can result in awareness of oneness with the object contemplated and direct realization of pure consciousness.

metaphysics Greek *meta*, beyond or after; *physika*, the physical side of Nature. The branch of philosophy that investigates the primary principles of ultimate reality, the nature of being, and the causes of the universe and its aspects and actions.

mind *Manas*, to think; hence the word *man*, thinker. The perception and information processing organ of human beings and creatures. Cosmic or Universal Mind and individualized minds are composed of cosmic forces regulated by the influences of the three primary attributes (*gunas*) of Nature.

moksha Also *mukti*. Liberation of soul consciousness. Liberation is accomplished when awareness is devoid of delusions and illusions. See *jivanmukta* and *salvation*.

mudra A symbolic gesture. Also, a yogic procedure used to regulate and enliven the body's life forces and to regulate or acquire mastery over involuntary processes.

nadi A channel or pathway through which prana flows in the body. *Ida* is the left channel along the spinal pathway, the lunar influence. *Pingala* is the right channel, the solar influence. The central channel is *sushumna*, the pathway through which the meditator directs vital forces when practicing certain Kriya Yoga meditation techniques or similar procedures. *Sushumna* is the outermost covering of two subtle astral channels, *vajra* and *chittra*. Within them is *brahmanadi*, described as "a current of consciousness." When awareness is identified with *vajra* and *chitra nadis*, one may have astral perceptions and experiences. When awareness is identified with *brahmanadi*, refined and transcendent samadhi states are possible.

nadi shuddhi Purification of the nadis by pranayama practice or when prana flows spontaneously after kundalini is awakened. See *nadi*, *prana*, and *pranayama*.

Nirguna-Brahma Supreme Consciousness without attributes or qualities. *Saguna-Brahma* is Supreme Consciousness expressing with attributes and qualities.

ojas The most refined form of energy-as-matter that strengthens and vitalizes body and mind and enhances awareness. The final product of food transformation, it is strengthened and increased by stress management, conservation and transmutation of physical and mental energies, mental calm, wholesome lifestyle routines, spiritual practices, and the cultivation of superconscious states. See *Ayurveda* and *brahmacharya*.

Om (*AUM*) The creative sound-current force emanating from the Godhead and from which all manifestations of Nature are produced. *Om* is the pure meditation mantra from which all other mantras derive their potencies.

omnipotence Unlimited power.

omnipresence Present everywhere.

omniscience All knowing.

paramahansa *Para*, beyond or transcendent; *hansa*, swan. One considered to be a spiritual master: a free soul no longer bound by rules because wisdom-impelled actions are always spontaneously appropriate. As a swan has an earthly abode and can soar free in the sky, so a paramahansa dwells in the world but is not influenced by or confined to it. According to mythology, a swan is able to extract milk from a mixture of milk and water. A paramahansa partakes of the divine essence while living without restrictions in the world.

Paramahansa Yogananda Disciple of Sri Yukteswar and the guru of Roy Eugene Davis. Born in India, January 5, 1893, he lived in America from 1920 until his *mahasamadhi* (conscious exit from the body) on March 7, 1952. His most famous book is *Autobiography of a Yogi*.

prakriti The primary field of Nature composed of subtle element influences and their manifestations and discernible characteristics. Prakriti is produced and enlivened by *Purusha*, the Supreme Being. See *maya*.

prana *Pra*, forth; *an*, to breathe. Life force. Its various aspects influence specific life-support functions. The soul's life force that vitalizes the body flows in through the medulla oblongata at the base of the brain. When prana flows freely, health prevails. When prana flows are weak or imbalanced, physical or psychological discomfort or dysfunction may occur. Pranayama practice harmonizes the flows of prana in the body and allows its expansion. The five aspects of prana in the body are: (1) *udana* (upward flowing), seated in the throat, it contributes to speech; (2) *prana*, seated in the chest, it regulates breathing; (3) *samana*, seated in the stomach and intestines, it regulates digestion, assimilation, and biochemical processes; (4) *apana*, seated below the navel, it regulates elimination of the body's waste products; (5) *vyana*, pervades the body and regulates the movements of other aspects of prana. See *pranayama* and *chakras*.

pranayama *Pran[a]*, life force; *ayama*, not restrained or freely flowing. Pranayama can occur naturally when the mind is calm, or be nurtured by pranayama practice. See *prana*.

primordial Nature Primary or original Nature. Om and its self-referring aspects: space, time, and cosmic forces with potential to express as objective Nature. See *prakriti*.

prayer Prayer can be verbal, mental, or the wordless aspiration of the heart (innermost being). Surrendered prayer purifies the ego, allowing apprehension of soul qualities and direct perception of transcendent realities. People of all faiths have experienced the transformational effects of surrendered prayer. Some have realized God by prayer alone, without knowledge or practice of other techniques or procedures. Petitioning prayer is the act of asking God for help or benefits of some kind, the results of which are demonstrated as satisfying states of consciousness or desired circumstances.

rasayana *Ras*, taste, juice, elixir, or essence; *ayana*, pathway, to circulate, or to have a home, place, or abode. In Ayurveda, it is a means of restoring the immune system and encouraging body fluids to circulate and be directed to their natural places. Herbal compounds prescribed for rasayana therapy are many and varied. One such preparation is *chyavanprash* (the food [*prash*] of a sage known as Chyavan who, according to a legendary story, used it to rejuvenate his body after being asked to marry a young woman who was in love with him). One recipe for chyavanprash includes a mixture of raw sugar, clarified butter, Indian gall nut, Indian gooseberry (amla fruit), dried catkins, Indian pennywort, honey, nutgrass, white sandalwood,

embrella, aloewood, licorice, cardamom, cinnamon, and tur-
meric. Ingredients may vary. See *Ayurveda* and *kaya-kalpa*.

reincarnation The doctrine of return: of being born into a physical body after a duration of rest in the astral realm. The belief
that the soul can be attracted to the physical realms because
its states of consciousness are compatible with them or because
of conscious or unconscious mental or emotional attachments.
Souls may also move from causal to astral realms. See *astral*
and *causal* realms.

renunciation Relinquishment of mental and emotional attachments to things, circumstances, emotional states, actions, and
the results of actions while dispassionately involved in relationships, activities, and spiritual practices.

sadhana From the verb-root *sadh*, to go straight to the goal.
Concentrated spiritual self-training and practice.

sage A wise person.

salvation The condition of being liberated from pain or discomfort because of Self-knowledge and the overcoming, removal,
or transcendence of karmic conditions, delusions, and illusions
by personal endeavor and God's grace. Limited salvation is a
confined condition: Self-realization may not be complete or
awareness may still be subject to the influences of subliminal
impressions. When awareness is removed from all influences
that formerly restricted it, liberation is absolute. See *moksha*.

samadhi From the verb-root *sam*, to put together. When mental modifications and fluctuations no longer fragment or disrupt awareness, samadhi (oneness or wholeness) is experienced.
Samadhi is a state of clarified awareness. Preliminary samadhi states may be mixed with thoughts, memories, emotions,
or fantasies. As mental transformations become less distract-

ing and are calmed, refined samadhi states unfold. Samadhi during which awareness is identified with and supported by an object of meditative contemplation (light, Om, or any other object of the meditator's attention) is conditional and temporary. Superconsciousness that removes one's awareness from objects is transcendent.

samkalpa Concentrated will or intention to cause a thing, event, or circumstance to manifest.

samkhya The system of philosophy in which the categories, stages, and orderly processes of cosmic manifestation from the field of pure Consciousness to the physical realm are defined, numbered, classified, and described. God, the Oversoul, emerges from the field of pure Consciousness. From God, a vibratory force (Om) is emanated. Om, interacting with its attributes (gunas) expresses as the field of primary Nature: space, time, and cosmic forces. God's Spirit or Life in relationship to the field of primordial Nature expresses as fields of individualized awareness, each referred to as a Self which, when identified with mind and matter, is referred to as a soul. The field of primordial Nature with the influences of its attributes projects Cosmic or Universal Mind, the essences of the five senses, the five organs or instrumental modes of action, and the fine essences of the five elements which further express as gross matter. A comprehensive understanding of Consciousness and how it expresses provides knowledge that one Reality, referring to and interacting only with itself, exists. Souls are individualized aspects of the one Consciousness in relationship to the emanated cosmic forces which comprise the field of Nature and its varied expressions. Because souls are aspects of one Consciousness, they need only to awaken to awareness of the truth of what they are.

samsara *Sam*, together; verb-root *sri*, to flow. Nature's continuous interactions and transformations occurring in the field of space-time. Unenlightened people involved in the currents of samsara are influenced by its actions. Enlightened souls established in Self-knowledge are not influenced by transitory events and circumstances.

samskara Mental impression, memory. Perceptions, whether of objective circumstances or of subjective incidents such as thoughts, feelings, or insights, impress the mind and are retained as memories. If influential, they can disturb mental and emotional peace by causing fluctuations and transformations in one's mind and awareness. They can have potential for pain or pleasure, or be neutral or constructive. Mental impressions made by superconscious influences are entirely constructive. Spiritual practices and superconscious states resist, weaken, and dissolve samskaras. See *karma*.

samyama Perfected meditative contemplation, accomplished when concentration, meditation, and identification with the object of contemplation are simultaneous.

Sanatana Dharma *Sanatana*, eternal; *dharma*, that which supports or upholds. The philosophical system that explains "the eternal way of righteousness"—the timeless and universally applicable way to live in accord with natural laws and evolutionary impulses which support orderliness, the welfare of all beings, the fulfillment of purposes, and rapid spiritual growth.

Sanskrit The refined, perfected, or polished language from which approximately one hundred Indo-European languages and English are derived. Prominent in India during the Vedic era and used today by some scholars and truth seekers. The Sanskrit alphabet is considered to be a mantra: a sound-phrase of spiritual significance and power which contains the seed-frequencies of creation. Every sound (*shabda*) has a power (*shakti*) which conveys the sense which is inseparably related to the sound. The sound-element behind the audible sound is the fundamental sound (*sphota*). Contemplation of the subtle sound-element or seed-power reveals its true essence. Sanskrit mantras are believed to be unique for the purpose of facilitating spiritual awakening. Their potency is derived from Om, the primordial sound current emanating from the Godhead and expressive throughout the universe. See *Om* and *mantra*.

sat Being, reality, truth, purity, luminosity. Consciousness with attributes is sometimes referred to by its characteristics, described as *Sat-Chit-Ananda*: Reality-Consciousness-Bliss of Being. See *guna*.

seer The Self, that which sees, perceives, or observes.

Self The soul's true essence of being. See *atman* and *soul*.

Self-realization Conscious knowledge-experience of one's true nature. The Self of every person and creature is pure consciousness. When identified with mental processes, the body, sensations, and sense objects, the Self becomes outwardly involved and partially forgets its real nature. Self-remembrance, orderly living, spiritual practice, and intellectual and intuitive analysis of one's true nature contribute to soul awakening and Self-realization: the restoration of awareness to its original, pure state.

shakti Cosmic creative force enlivening nature. Also, the energies of awakened kundalini which vitalize the body and quicken psychological transformation and spiritual growth.

shaktipat The transmission of creative force from one person to another, usually from the guru to a disciple; also its spontaneous awakening because of sustained aspiration to enlightenment, devotion, spiritual practices, and grace.

siddha One who is spiritually perfected or accomplished.

siddhi Siddhis are innate powers and abilities which become available to one who is spiritually perfected or accomplished. Although they can be used to accomplish purposes of all kinds, they should primarily be used to accomplish liberation.

soul An individualized ray of the one Consciousness reflected from the field of primordial Nature that mistakenly presumes itself to be independent of God. The soul's illusional state of awareness has to be purified and transcended to be restored to wholeness. See *salvation*, *moksha*, and *jivanmukta*.

spiritual eye The reflected light from the medulla oblongata at the base of the brain inwardly perceived between and behind the eyebrows. The meditator directs attention to and through the spiritual eye to have subtle perceptions and to explore refined states of consciousness.

Sri Yukteswar Disciple of Lahiri Mahasaya and the guru of Paramahansa Yogananda. (May 10, 1855–March 9, 1936.)

superconscious A clarified state of awareness superior to conscious, subconscious, and unconscious states. See *turiya*.

swami A member of the ancient monastic order reorganized by the philosopher-seer Adi (the first) Shankara in the seventh century. A swami renounces all mundane attachments, selflessly works for the highest good of others, and (usually) engages in spiritual practices to awaken to God-realization.

tantra From *tan*, to extend or expand. Tantric philosophy explains the processes of creation and dissolution of the cosmos, procedures for relating to universal forces and accomplishing the aims of life, how to awaken and express innate abilities, and meditation techniques to clear the mind and facilitate awakening to ultimate Truth-realization.

tapasya From the verb-root *tap*, to burn. Concentrated practices that facilitate psychological transformation and remove restrictions to spiritual growth and Self-actualization.

tattva The true essence of a thing which can be known by practicing samyama: meditative contemplation.

Transcendental Field Pure Consciousness, the Absolute.

turiya The fourth state of consciousness transcending the three commonly experienced states of deep sleep, the dream state, and ordinary waking states. See *superconscious*.

Upanishads *Upa*, near; *ni*, down; *sad*, to sit. A collection of texts considered sacred, with origins in oral traditions. Centuries ago, in India, the disciple would live in the guru's ashram and sit near him or her to learn. Among the several Upanishads, the ones which are more widely published are referred to as the principle ones because of their general accessibility. Other little known Upanishads contain specific yogic instruction. One such text, the *Shandilya Upanishad*, was written by an ancestor of Lahiri Mahasaya.

vasana Latent tendency, subconscious sensation which can cause thought-waves to arise in the mind, mental transformations, and fluctuations in awareness. They can be neutralized by constructive living, spiritual practices, and superconsciousness (samadhi). See *vritti*.

veda Revealed knowledge. Vedic texts are records of insights of ancient seers; the Upanishads elaborate on the Vedas.

Vedanta The summing up of the wisdom of the Vedas. The final revelation is that one Consciousness is the cause, reality, and support of all that is.

vritti Movement, wave, fluctuation, or modification occurring in the mind and awareness impelled by *vasanas* (impulses of the subliminal tendencies of samskaras) which stir them into motion. Vrittis are calmed by dispassionate observation of circumstances and by meditation practiced to the stage of superconsciousness. See *vasana*.

Vyasa A name used by several ancient sages who "gathered" and arranged many of the Vedic texts.

yama-niyama *Yama*, restraint. By resisting and regulating destructive impulses, their opposite characteristics are cultivated and perfected: harmlessness; truthfulness; honesty; constructive use of vital forces and soul capacities; and insightful renunciation which makes possible appropriate relationships and prudent use of natural resources. *Niyama*, not-restraint, the constructive actions: maintaining inner and outer cleanliness or purity; soul contentment in all circumstances; disciplined practices to facilitate psychological transformation (*tapasya*); study and meditation to awaken to Self-knowledge and contemplation of higher realities; surrender of the illusional sense of independent selfhood in favor of awakening to awareness and realization of transcendent realities.

yantra A symbolic, geometrical drawing depicting the actions and influences of cosmic forces, used as a focus for meditative contemplation. Favored by many yogis is *Sri Yantra*, composed of circles, triangles, lotus petals, and mantras within a square form to contain the energies. The design portrays the interactions of *Shiva* and *Shakti*: Supreme Consciousness and its cosmic creative Power and energies.

yoga 1. To "yoke" or "unify," to bring together; to identify one's awareness with the One Consciousness by using specific practices that remove restrictions from mind and awareness. 2. Any of the various systems used for this purpose. 3. Samadhi is the meaning used in Patanjali's Yoga-Sutras.

Practices vary in accord with the psychological temperament and personal capacities of the devotee. *Hatha Yoga* practitioners endeavor to control physiological and psychological states by the application of asanas (postures), pranayamas, mudras, and meditative practices. *Bhakti Yoga* is the devotional approach to apprehending the all-pervading reality of God. *Karma Yoga* is the way of mental and emotional renunciation of the results of actions rather than the avoidance of the performance of necessary actions. *Jnana* (gy-ana) *Yoga* is the way of intentional use of powers of discriminative intelligence to discern the truth of Self, God, and Nature. *Raja* (royal, kingly) *Yoga* is the eightfold way of perfecting: (1) the five external disciplines; (2) the five internal disciplines; (3) meditation posture; (4) pranayama, to master life forces and mental processes; (5) internalization of attention; (6) concentration; (7) meditation; (8) superconscious states. The terms Kriya Yoga, Kundalini Yoga, Laya Yoga, and others that are sometimes used, indicate specialized practices found within the basic systems.

Yoga-Sutras A concise treatise on yoga philosophy and practice written by Patanjali in which Kriya Yoga procedures are described. See *Part Two*.

yuga An Age, Era, or designated duration of time. Centuries ago, vedic astronomer-seers taught a theory of time-cycles to explain the effects of cosmic forces on human beings and evolutionary trends that affect Planet Earth. The ascending cycle is one-half of a complete 24,000-year cycle: (1) a 1,200-year Dark Age (*Kali Yuga*) during which most human beings are intellectually deficient and spiritually unaware; (2) the second

(*Dwapara Yuga*) 2,400-year era during which intellectual powers and spiritual awareness increase and electric and magnetic
properties of Nature are discovered anew; (3) the third (*Treta*)
3,600-year era when intellectual powers are keen and knowledge of Nature's forces is common; (4) the 4,800-year era of enlightenment (*Satya*, truth-knowledge) during which many on
the planet can comprehend the reality of God. We are currently
in the early stages of a second ascending 2,400-year Age which
emerged in 1700 and will continue until the year 4,100, when
the 3,600-year ascending Mental Age will begin. The duration
of the Ages, in ascending order, are actually 1,000, 2,000, 3,000,
and 4,000 solar years. An additional ten percent of the duration of each Age begins and ends each transition phase.

The calculation of time-cycles is based on the theory that forces
from the center of our galaxy influence the electromagnetic field
of the solar system and the mental and intellectual faculties of
its human inhabitants. When our solar system is distant from
the galactic center, human powers of perception are weak,
intellectual powers are minimal, soul awareness is obscured,
and ignorance of the facts of life prevail. When our Sun and its
planets are nearest to the galactic center, human powers of perception are refined, intellectual abilities are pronounced, soul
knowledge is more easily unveiled, and various degrees of
enlightenment are common. Regardless of the Age in which one
lives, when aspiration to Self-discovery is impelling, spiritual
growth that culminates in illumination of consciousness is possible. One can choose to awaken from identification with characteristics which are common to the individual deluded condition to the stage which makes possible comprehension of fine
forces behind the outer appearance of Nature. At this stage one
can appreciate the philosophical principles upon which Kriya
Yoga practices are based and be motivated to right living and
spiritual endeavor. Further awakening enables one to apprehend and effectively relate to Cosmic Mind. The final awaken-

ing is the result of spontaneous revelation of innate knowledge.

Because of a mistake that was made several centuries ago (circa 700 BCE) in calculating the progressions of the yugas, many people still believe that we are currently in a Dark Age cycle that will continue for several hundred thousand years. The error occurred near the end of the last descending Dwapara Yuga. Astrologers, not wanting to inform the public about the impending emergence of two consecutive Dark Ages (a 1,200 year descending era followed by an ascending era of equal duration) proclaimed that the Dwapara Yuga would continue. Much later, the mistake was noted, but its cause was not then known.

Observation of the present state of collective human consciousness, and of scientific discoveries and technological advances made during the past few hundred years, will reveal that we are in a time-period of rapid intellectual and spiritual awakening which is characteristic of an emerging Dwapara Yuga.

About the Author

One of the few remaining direct disciples of Paramahansa Yogananda, Roy Eugene Davis is a proficient teacher of the soul-liberating practices of Kriya Yoga.

Born in 1931 near Warren, Ohio, Mr. Davis began his spiritual quest at an early age. After reading Paramahansa Yogananda's book, *Autobiography of a Yogi*, in 1949, he traveled to Los Angeles, California, to meet his guru. After two years of discipleship training and intensive spiritual practice, he was ordained by Yogananda in 1951.

Since then, he has lectured and presented meditation seminars throughout North America and in Japan, Brazil, Europe, England, West Africa, and India. Some of his many books have been published in Japanese, German, Spanish, Portuguese, Italian, Turkish, and Chinese languages. Several English language editions are published in India.*

*Motilal Banarsidass Publishers, 41 U.A., Bungalow Road, Jawahar Nagar, Delhi 110 007.

B. Jain Publishers, P.O. Box 5775, New Delhi 110 055

Center For Spiritual Awareness

Our teaching emphasis is that it is possible for every aspiring person to unfold and express their innate potential and live a fulfilled life in harmony with natural laws.

CSA's international headquarters is located in the quiet, secluded mountain region of northeast Georgia. Facilities include the administrative offices and publishing department, five guest houses, the main meditation hall and dining room, the Shrine of All Faiths Meditation Temple, two library buildings, and a book store. Weekend and week long meditation retreats are offered at CSA headquarters on a regular schedule. Roy Eugene Davis is the spiritual director.

A free information packet and book catalog
may be requested from the address below:

Center For Spiritual Awareness
Lake Rabun Road, P.O. Box 7
Lakemont, Georgia 30552-0007 (U.S.A.)

(706) 782-4723 weekdays, 8 a.m. – 4 p.m.
Fax (706) 782-4560
E-mail csa@stc.net   Web Site www.csa-davis.org